Author and pastor A. K. Fuller br
bite-sized chunks while retainin
personal anecdotes, self-depre
Fuller connects the dots of th

of Scripture in engaging, accessible ways. Whether one is a new explorer or a veteran of Biblical studies, *Overall* offers the reader a fresh look at the central motif of God's amazing (and patient!) interaction with us carbon-based bipeds.

Dave Workman, President of The Elemental Group and author of *The Outward Focused Life* and *Elemental Leaders: Four Essentials Every Leader Needs...and Every Church Must Have*

With the creativity of a storyteller, the insight of a scholar, and the quirk of a friend you'd love to laugh with over a latte, A. K. Fuller welcomes us into a journey through the Bible, church history, and our own messy lives in his new book *Overall*. This engaging overview of the Christian faith helps readers gain a better understanding of God's story and celebrate our own unique place within it. Having been a book reviewer for over thirty years, I've read a lot of Christian titles, and honestly, this is one of the best.

Vicki Kuyper, author of *Wonderlust* and *A Tale of Two Biddies*

A. K. Fuller takes a wrecking ball to the myth that the Christian life is deep and therefore complex. Fuller supplied me with new ways of seeing the simply profound truth of the *Overall* story of Christianity. If you're hungry for God and yearn for spiritual depth, the template is here.

Steve Sjogren, author of *Conspiracy of Kindness*

Overall is absolutely incredible. It's one of the best overviews of the story of God and humanity that I have ever read. It is a must-read for anyone curious about Jesus and for those who have followed Jesus their whole lives. Fuller's ability to explain the overarching story of the Bible with illustrations and metaphors that the reader can easily relate to makes the book both readable and accessible. As you read the book, the stories of the Bible come alive as they are understood within the context of The Story. Fuller's style of writing draws readers in and keeps them engaged. With each chapter, the overall narrative of what God is doing and our role in the story become more and more compelling. This book is for everyone. The skeptic and the believer. The churched and the unchurched. Those who have never read the Bible and the biblical scholar. The one hearing the Word and the one preaching the Word. It's rare to find a book about the Bible that I can enthusiastically recommend to such a wide audience. This is one of those books.

Rod Stafford, Pastor of Fairfax Church and author of *Free to Lead*

A. K. Fuller is that rare mix of logic and art, of mathematics (his undergrad major) and creative genius. One of the finest teachers and preachers I know, he has clothed the sweeping narrative of the Bible, from Genesis to Revelation, with astonishing clarity, insight, and a weave that a world without the Word can grasp, digest, and apply. Fuller connects the dots for those in church and for those who have never darkened the door. Fun, smart, and rock-solid, *Overall* is, in fact, itself epic. More than a great read, this book will teach, preach, inspire, and transform. Grab a copy and be amazed. Beginning to end. By the Bible—and its central figure, Jesus.

Jim Lyon, General Director of Church of God Ministries,
author of *Go Ahead Ask Anything*

Overall is a triumph. Within the first pages it sets out its ambitious agenda to provide "a brief overview of human existence" and more specifically "to help us understand and feel more confident with the Overall Christian story." In the pages that follow, Pastor Fuller delivers. This is a book for people who are familiar with Christianity as a faith tradition and those who are curious, but who may not have put the whole story into context. Using a sensible structure and "aw-shucks" humor throughout, Fuller leads the reader through the biblical journey to the key end point: God loves us and we have the opportunity to have a real, life-changing relationship with him through Jesus Christ. This is the message of hope for us as individuals, for our families, communities, and nation. I highly recommend this wonderful book.

Mark Stoleson, Chief Executive Officer and Partner at Legatum

Overall: Understanding the Epic Christian Story is a book many of us in ministry have been waiting for. Fuller has a brilliant mind and the unique ability to understand the deeper truths of the Bible and how to apply them to our everyday lives. This book will be one you will want to share with others. You will find it difficult to put down. I predict that you, like me, will feel as if we are reading our own stories that we have been unable to process or share so eloquently.

Marty Grubbs, Pastor of Crossings Community Church
and author of *Restored*

Overall is an inspiring look at the grand stories that make up the Bible and summarizes them as the epic love story of God for his people. Fuller effectively uses humor, pop-culture references, and personal insights to shed light on how we can understand the story and shape our own. As a Catholic Christian, I found *Overall* insightful and encouraging. It serves as a great framework for those who want to learn more about the story and their place in it.

Jason Sauer, software developer and founder of Software Solutions

OVERALL

Understanding the Epic Christian Story

by A. K. Fuller

Warner Press, Inc.

Warner Press and Warner Press logo are trademarks of Warner Press, Inc.

Overall: Understanding the Epic Christian Story

Written by A. K. Fuller

Requests for information should be sent to:

Warner Press, Inc.
2902 Enterprise Drive
Anderson, IN 46013

www.warnerpress.org

Editor: Kevin Stiffler

Cover and Layout: Curtis Corzine

ISBN: 9781684344710

warner press®

To Rita Puckett—

Thank you for raising a precious daughter,
for modeling love and generosity to your grandkids,
and for enduring years of mother-in-law jokes.

Table Of Contents

Before We Begin

Nobody wants to feel stupid.

Nobody enjoys that moment at the auto repair shop when you get to the counter and they ask, "What seems to be the problem?"

Do you try to imitate the sound of the engine with your voice? For the mechanic behind the counter, I imagine that's more of a job perk than a helpful diagnostic tool.

Do you admit you don't know where the smoke is coming from because you couldn't figure out how to open the hood? Or do you just hand over the keys and pretend you didn't understand the question?

Then you have to make decisions based on their recommendations: "Your water pump needs to be replaced, but we can save you *money* if we replace the timing belt while we're in there because that *sucker* is hard to get to. We'll also check to see if you *broke* any valves or damaged any pistons."

All you hear is, "Blah blah blah...*money*...blah blah blah...*sucker*... blah blah blah...*broke*."

Nobody wants to feel stupid at the hardware store, or at the counter at Starbucks, or at the workout machines at the gym.

And nobody wants to feel stupid in church.

The pastor/minister/priest gets up and says, "At this time we are going to eat the body of Christ and drink the cup that is the blood of the covenant."

What did he say?

"The Eucharist is a reminder of Christ's atoning sacrifice so that we can be justified for our sins and sanctified through the ongoing work of the Holy Spirit."

What? I thought Euchre was a card game we used to play in Indiana.

Later, the pastor/minister/priest shares a joke that was found on the Internet: "Remember—before Boaz was married, he was Ruth-less!"

People around you snicker. You look at them with your eyebrows raised and a slight smile, pretending you understand the reference. You assume you're the only one in the room who doesn't get it, but you're wrong. The room is *filled* with people who are pretending because they, like you, don't want to feel stupid in church.

Pile of Lumber

This book is a brief overview of human existence, broken down into seven parts. Its purpose is to help us understand and feel more confident with the Overall Christian story. It's an attempt to see and appreciate the proverbial "forest," instead of getting frustrated by the confusing and endless "trees."

Imagine every chapter, every verse, every parable, every idea from the Bible that you are familiar with is a two-by-four piece of wood. All those two-by-fours are now laid out on the ground and create a pile of lumber. For some, the pile is small. You didn't grow up attending church; you don't know the stories; you don't get the Boaz joke. For others, it's a rather massive pile of lumber—all mixed up and scattered on the ground.

Now, imagine adding two-by-fours for every notable moment in human history and every significant story in *your* life. That's a huge pile of wood. How do they all fit together?

Many people are passionate about the two particular pieces of wood that form the cross. They know the story of Jesus and many of the things he did and said, but how do those pieces fit with the Noah-and-the-ark two-by-four or the Muslim two-by-four?

This book is an attempt to take all that wood and build a framework for a beautiful and understandable structure. In the following pages, we will not just look at individual stories—we will be looking at the Overall story of humanity. This is important because the story we believe we are living in shapes how we live our lives.

People who call themselves "Trekkers" would know who Khan is. They might even go to conventions and speak Klingon. They would know the *Star Trek* story.

People who call themselves "gearheads" would hop under the car to take a look no matter what they were wearing or where they were headed. They wouldn't imitate sounds to a mechanic at the repair shop.

If I call myself a "Christian," isn't it reasonable to expect that I would know the Christian story? The overall percentage is declining, but most Americans still identify themselves as Christian—most, as in more than 150 million people. But how many of these know the Overall story?

People in church don't want to feel stupid. They don't want to stare at a confusing pile of lumber. They want to know God's story and how they fit into it.

Framework

I love structure. I'm a math guy. I remember when the world of calculus opened for me in high school. It was beautiful. I finally saw how the arithmetic pieces, and the geometric pieces, and the algebraic pieces, and the trigonometric pieces all fit together. Math was no longer irrelevant and isolated operations, repeated ad nauseam. It was all part of a grand and beautiful framework.

Okay, maybe that's why I didn't date many girls in high school.

I grew up in Canada in a non-Christian home located across the street from a small, loving church. The people at that church invited my brothers and me to attend, and my parents were happy to get a few weekly hours of silence. Over time, I learned multiple stories from the Bible, imprinted into my brain through the high-tech cutouts that would stick to the flannel boards.[1] I became familiar with bits and pieces (two-by-fours), but I had no concept of the grand story (framework).

I tried to read the Bible because I was told it was critical for those who follow Jesus. I read the Book of Genesis about seventeen times, but significantly slowed down in the Book of Exodus when they repeated the details of the tabernacle. And getting through Leviticus was about as likely as me reading Shakespeare "just for fun."

I had so many debilitating questions:

- How could Moses write the creation story when he wasn't alive until many years later?
- Where do the dinosaurs fit?
- How could Moses have written about his own death and how the people responded after he died?
- Why are there two versions of the stories of King Saul and King David? And why does the second version omit David's mistake with Bathsheba?
- Why do so many of the psalms sound like whining and complaining?

So I set the Bible down and went back to watching hockey.

Years later, I sensed a call to full-time ministry and attended seminary in Anderson, Indiana. One course was a survey of the Book of Romans. There were twenty students in the class, and the professor assigned each of us a different commentary (a book that provides interpretive explanation). We walked through the chapters in Romans and compared what the commentary writers had to say about each chapter. The professor would look around the room and say something such as, "Fuller, what did Schleiermacher think about Romans 1:17?"

I walked away with a degree but still had no sense of the Overall story. I dove deep into the minutiae of biblical languages and proper formatting for bibliographies, but I had no sense of the big picture. Lots of lumber; no framework.

My first full-time ministry job was at Vineyard Community Church in Cincinnati, Ohio. It was an honor to be part of a team that was doing radical acts of kindness as a demonstration of God's love—and passionately singing simple love songs to Jesus. It was new, it was beautiful, it was life-changing. But in terms of understanding the grand

Christian story—more lumber, no framework.

Years later, I became the lead pastor of a church in Phoenix, Arizona. This provided me with the opportunity to start building a framework for the biblical story based on seven parts that run from creation through the end of time. In the congregation I served, we committed an entire year to walking this out. I enjoyed it so much that I did it again year after year, looking at different themes that run through the Overall story.

The seven parts of this framework form the structure of this book. Parts I and II summarize the Old Testament, and Parts III and IV cover the New Testament. Overviews of the Bible typically stop there, but the story does not. Part V zooms quickly through the two thousand years that connect the story of the Bible with our own. I consider Part VI to be the most miraculous one: God is not just inviting us to learn the story—he[2] is inviting us *into* the story. Then the final part looks at glimpses God has given us of the end of the story.

This book is somewhat of a *Choose Your Own Adventure.* If you feel rather solid about the Bible story, perhaps it would be best to jump to Part V and see how the story continues after the Bible. If you eagerly want to get to the most important part, skip to Part III and discover Jesus, the greatest two-by-four in the pile. If you're ready to explore the Overall story…clip on your toolbelt, and grab a hammer. Let's turn some lumber into framework.

---

1. The use of flannelgraphs used to be common practice in church classrooms to provide visuals that helped with learning. The first iPad, perhaps?
2. God is not male. Men and women are both created in God's image, and God demonstrates both masculine and feminine characteristics. God is God, and God is not bound by gender as we are. Throughout this book, I will use masculine pronouns for God due to the limitations of the English language, and for ease of reading.

PART I:
ONE NATION

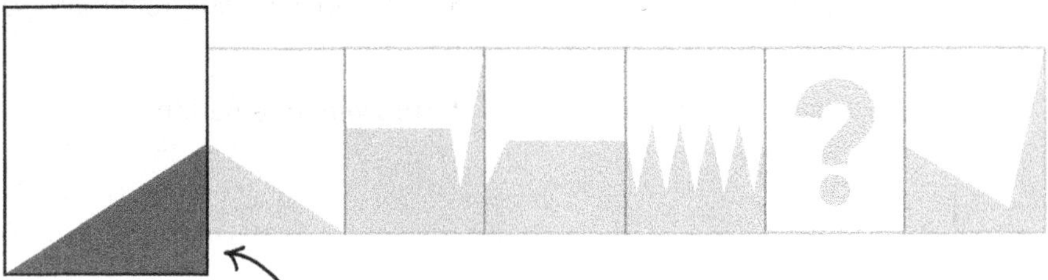

One Nation: the growth and development of Israel

Intro

You gotta start somewhere.

George Lucas started with a protocol droid and his beeping sidekick. Pixar started with a hopping lamp. J. K. Rowling started with a delusional family on Privet Drive.

The beginning of an epic story is exciting. You're introduced to the main characters one at a time, knowing you're about to spend many hours with them and hoping you will enjoy the experience and be affected by it.

God started with a nation.

The Bible consists of two sections. The first and much larger section is called the Old Testament. It includes everything up until the birth of Jesus. It's the history of the world from the perspective of one chosen group of people in a region east of the Mediterranean where Europe, Africa, and Asia meet.

To begin, we will assemble framework that represents the first half of the Old Testament story. It's the story of God identifying a man who became a family that became a nation. It chronicles the growth of the ancient biblical nation of Israel as they developed from wandering desert-dwellers into a powerful empire.

The Old Testament is important because it lays the foundation for the story of Jesus. He arrived at a certain moment in history, and it's critical to step back and discover the story that set things up for that moment.

The Old Testament is also important because Jesus read it and endorsed it. Imagine your copy of the Old Testament with a quote from Jesus on the front cover: "I read it. I loved it. I highly recommend it!"

You gotta start somewhere. God started with one nation.

1.1 Setting the Stage

The greatest day of my oldest son's life was May 4, 2012.

That Thursday morning, I surprised Gordon at school by taking him out of his fifth-grade class at 11 AM. We drove to a movie theater nearby where I handed him his lanyard that gave him access to a marathon of Marvel movies that would crescendo into the first showing of *The Avengers* at 12:01 AM that night.

I have made numerous mistakes as Gordon's dad. This was not one of them.

We had a blast as we spent fifteen uninterrupted hours filling our stomachs with all-you-can-eat soda and popcorn, and filling our retinas with Marvel Cinematic Universe magic.

Watching all the movies in a row was tremendously helpful for me because I was lost in the sea of superhero characters. Movies would end and we would remain in our seats through the rolling credits (a practice I had not done since *Ferris Bueller's Day Off*). Then a mysterious creature would appear in a short scene and the Marvel-maniacs in the theatre would explode with excitement. I would lean over to my son and say, "Who's that? What did that person do?" I was very confused.

I didn't grow up reading Marvel comics. I wasn't even familiar with Iron Man at all.

Blasphemy, I know.

I had seen *The Iron Giant*, which I considered to be a terrific movie, but I had little interest in the smaller version. I mean, how many stories can there be about a character in an iron suit?

By the time *The Avengers* started I was nearly sick to my stomach, but my mind was aware of the unfolding epic story and the multitude of major characters.

I'm sure a day involving my son's future wife or kids will take over the top spot in his life, but as of this writing, May 4, 2012, remains the winner.

For many, the Old Testament can feel confusing because there are so many characters to keep track of. We hear a name referred to in a sermon at church and we want to lean over to someone and ask, "Who's that? What did that person do?"

The whole story starts with the *Adam and Eve* "movie," which is the account of a young couple who were part of an exclusive nudist colony until they ate the forbidden fruit. Then there's the *Noah* movie, where God chooses to restart human existence. Among others, we have *Jacob* the persistent husband, *Joseph* the patient dreamer, and *Joshua* the orbiting warrior.

So many characters...so many stories...so many two-by-fours. It's difficult to keep track.

Three Main Characters

It might be helpful to break the story down into three main characters—not just for the story of the ancient nation of Israel but for the grand story of human existence.

Main Character #1: God

The first and main character of the Overall story is introduced in Genesis 1, the first chapter of the Bible:

> *In the beginning God created the heavens and the earth.*
> *—Genesis 1:1*[1]

These ten words set the tone for the entire narrative of the Bible. It certainly takes faith to embrace them, but no more faith than it takes to believe that a living cell could somehow form from nothing on a planet that somehow had all the precise criteria for life to exist. The rest of Genesis 1 is a poem about the seven days of creation. There's much debate on what exactly happened on each of the days, or how long they were, but we won't be able to experience the fullness of the story unless we can embrace these first ten words.

God is not just the Creator; he's the protagonist and hero of the story. He should be on the front cover of the book and on the promotional posters for the movie. We find out later that God takes the form of three persons: Father, Son, and Holy Spirit—all of whom are present in the opening chapter of the Bible.

Main Character #2: Us

You and I are the second main character in the story. We're introduced in Genesis 2:

> *Then the* Lord *God formed a man from the dust of the ground and breathed into his nostrils the breath of life.* —Genesis 2:7

The Overall story is a love story, really. Humanity is the crown of God's creation and the object of his affection. His aim is not to manage us and reduce the mistakes we make; he wants to spend eternity with us. He doesn't want us simply to obey him out of fear; he wants us to willingly love him back.

Main Character #3: Satan

In the third chapter of Genesis, we're introduced to the antagonist:

> *Now the serpent was more crafty than any of the wild animals the* Lord *God had made.* —Genesis 3:1

There's much we don't know about Satan. There's no evidence that he has horns, or that his skin has a reddish tone, or that he's a gifted fiddle player. The traditional story is that he was a high-ranking angel named Lucifer who was gifted with freedom of choice. He was not satisfied with being subservient to God, so he rebelled and was banished from heaven along with one third of the heavenly beings who sided with him. Most of our impressions of Satan come more from tradition and writings such as Milton's "Paradise Lost" than from the Bible.

What we do know is that Satan is evil and is hell-bent on sabotaging the relationship between the first two characters. He knows he's no match for God, so his plan is to go after what God cares most about: you and me. From Genesis 3 through the end of the story, the enemy is present and active. The Overall narrative is both a love story *and* an epic battle of good versus evil.

Two Levels

I would like to jump to another book in the Old Testament entitled Job. It's a drama centered around the three main characters, and it provides an intriguing perspective on the framework of the Overall story. The reader is exposed to an interaction between God and Satan that has horrific impact on a man named Job. It's as if we are the audience watching a drama unfold on a stage that has two levels.

On the upper level we find the supernatural stage. This is the realm of God and the angels. This is where we see Satan trying to drive a wedge between God and Job. Satan says that Job is only faithful because God has provided Job with a family and everything he might desire. He claims that Job's love for God is an immature love, sort of like a child expressing love at Christmas by saying, "Santa is great because he gave me everything I wanted! Mom and Dad are okay, but Santa is amazing!" Satan (no relation to Santa, despite the anagram) believes if he is allowed to take everything away from Job, then Job will abandon his relationship with God. This is a big deal. If Satan is correct in his declaration before God on the supernatural stage, then God's entire design is flawed because true, authentic love between the first two characters is not possible. The entire story rests on this moment. And God bets it all on Job.

On the lower level we find the reality stage. This is the story of humanity, the story that you and I get to live in. It's on this stage that we see Job lose his livestock, his wealth, his family, and his health. The characters on the upper level get to see the full picture of what's going on, whereas Job only has access to the lower level. And this remains the reality for you and me as the story of life continues to play out. We have access to the reality (lower) stage, but only glimpses of the supernatural (upper) stage.

Job's friends are, of course, limited to the lower level as well. At first they respond with grace and compassion. They are exemplary friends amid tragedy:

> *They set out from their homes and met together by agreement to go and sympathize with [Job] and comfort him.... They sat on the ground with him for seven days and seven nights. No one said a word. —Job 2:11, 13*

Sometimes the best thing to say to a hurting friend is nothing. Just be there.

But then we have thirty-six chapters of Job's friends drifting from compassion to condemnation. Three verses of grace, and 863 verses of judgment.[2] Sadly, that's a comparable ratio to what many of us experience. In the friends' defense, they were trying to rationally comprehend their limited-reality (lower) stage. There must have been some explanation for Job's misfortune because good people experience prosperity—and wicked people experience suffering. Job must have been more wicked than he or his friends once believed. This is logical. It makes sense.

Sometimes life doesn't follow a logical pattern and we have questions similar to those of Job's friends:

- Why did one person grow up without a dad, while someone else had both loving parents yet wanted nothing to do with them?
- Why did she end up with the unfaithful husband, but her friend, who was relationally irresponsible throughout college, ended up with an incredible spouse?
- Why did he lose his job after making a bold decision of integrity, but the other guy fenagled his way into a promotion?

There is no logical explanation, and a trite "spiritual" answer can do more harm than good. It doesn't mean our decisions are meaningless or our circumstances are random. It means there's more going on around us than we are aware of. There's a second level, a supernatural stage to which we do not have full access.

One Story

Like a disgruntled employee or a raging fan of a losing team, we sometimes think we can do a better job than the people in charge. From our limited perspective, we may even think God could have used our help in the development of his story. We like this part but not that part. We study these scenes but avoid those. We like the loving God of the New Testament but not the vengeful God of the Old Testament. We pick and choose our way through the Bible and imagine how God could have done his universe-creating job more effectively.

Job and his friends go back and forth through chapter 37, trying to explain why Job had such a horrific experience. Then the protagonist speaks from the upper stage:

> *"Where were you when I laid the earth's foundation?" —Job 38:4*

God goes on to engage in a four-chapter "dad speech" that is one of the greatest sections in all of the Scriptures. Most dads have a button, and when that button is pressed, they launch into a dad speech. When any of my kids say, "It's not fair," the others look at each another and say, "Uh oh."

" 'It's not fair'? Whoever told you life was supposed to be fair? Where did you get the impression that our relationship was fair? How many times have you bought groceries or paid the mortgage? Trust me, dear one, you don't want 'fair'!"

Every dad has a button. Some have several. Something Job and his friends said pushed God's button:

> *"What is the way to the place where the lightning is dispersed, or the place where the east winds are scattered over the earth?" —Job 38:24*

I smile when God gets a little saucy. Perhaps there's a shed somewhere that contains all the thunder and lightning, and God accesses that shed whenever there's a need.

God poetically describes the amazing diversity among the animals:

> *"The wings of the ostrich flap joyfully,*
> *though they cannot compare*
> *with the wings and feathers of the stork.*
> *She lays her eggs on the ground*
> *and lets them warm in the sand,*
> *unmindful that a foot may crush them,*
> *that some wild animal may trample them.*
> *She treats her young harshly, as if they were not hers;*
> *she cares not that her labor was in vain,*
> *for God did not endow her with wisdom*
> *or give her a share of good sense.*
> *Yet when she spreads her feathers to run,*
> *she laughs at horse and rider." —Job 39:13–18*

The ostrich is a goofy-looking animal. So is the naked mole rat. And the pink fairy armadillo. And Steven Tyler. Do we really think we could have done better? Are we really in a position to question the Designer?

God reminds Job that the beauty and variety of creation continues without Job's help. There are wild oxen that will never plow a field, and wild donkeys that will never be tame, and mountain goats that will give birth in secret places that will never be seen. There are amazing insects, animals, and sea creatures that have not yet been discovered and may never be. There are adorable offspring of all sorts of animals that will never be enjoyed by any human. Nature shows on television remain popular because they offer a glimpse of a world that remains inaccessible to most of us. In a beautiful and poetic way, God made it clear that we are not his equal, and we are not his peer. It is ignorant and arrogant of us to think we could ever stand toe-to-toe with the protagonist of the story—the one who laid the very foundations of the earth.

The question is not, "What parts of God's story do I like or believe?" The question is, "Do I believe this is the one, true story?" The whole thing, not just the parts I like. The Overall story is not a myth or a fable. It's not an ancient explanation of human life that merits our respect. And the story of human life is not whatever you and I wish it to be. There is one story of human existence. It's the story of a beautiful and intimate relationship between the first two characters and a third, evil character who wants to destroy that union.

Three main characters. Two levels. One story.

Blast off.

---

1. To clarify, whenever the format "#:#" is used, it is a reference to a Bible verse, such as Genesis 1:1. However, when the format "#.#" is used (period rather than colon), it is a reference to a chapter in this book, such as Chapter 1.1.

2. To be fair, Job spoke 487 of those verses while his three friends spoke 376, but many of Job's words were in response to the foolishness of his friends.

1.2 Five Hundred Yards

Years ago, my wife and I had the great pleasure of visiting the Holy Land. The most impactful thing for me was walking on the actual ground that characters in the Bible walked on.

"This...is the Kidron Valley—I'm literally walking in the 'valley of the shadow of death' from Psalm 23!"

"This...is where Solomon's temple was built!"

"This...is the floor of one of the synagogues Jesus may have attended!"

Eventually, my wife requested I enjoy these moments without yelling these phrases out.

The stories in the Bible are true. These were real people making world-altering decisions while standing on actual pieces of dirt. They weren't in Middle-earth, or Narnia, or "a galaxy far, far away." We can visit these real places, walk through these locations, and let the soil run through our fingers.

In the words of Han Solo when he first met a wide-eyed Rey, "It's true—all of it. It's all true."[1]

Abraham

One of these true stories is about a man named Abraham, who became the father of the ancient nation of Israel. God told him,

> *"I will make you into a great nation,*
> *and I will bless you;*
> *I will make your name great,*
> *and you will be a blessing."* —*Genesis 12:2*

This promise became an issue because he and his wife, Sarah, were not able to have children. At the ripe old age of one hundred, Abraham was told by God he would finally have a son. When ninety-year-old Sarah heard this, she laughed, which is why they named their son *Isaac*, which means, "one who laughs."

When the long-awaited and cherished boy grew to be a young man, God commanded Abraham to sacrifice his son on an altar.

I know, I know! This is one of those moments that make people not want to read the Bible. It is one of many examples, particularly in the Old Testament, where the limited view from the lower stage is excruciating. It's an awful story, but it's important to see both levels of the stage and understand that sacrifice was common at that time.

Almost every religion practiced some sort of sacrifice. It was considered a way to appease or please the gods. The sacrifice was usually food or animals, or even, at times, humans. To our modern minds, this is ridiculously barbaric. But Abraham lived in a world that did not yet have the laws of God. He did not yet know he was serving a God who would not require him to provide a human sacrifice. He was faithful, even with that which was most precious to him.

Abraham took his son to the foot of Mount Moriah. He asked his servants to stay and mind the donkey while he and Isaac climbed up to the altar at the top of the mountain:

> *Abraham took the wood for the burnt offering and placed it on his son Isaac, and he himself carried the fire and the knife. —Genesis 22:6*

They had many items, which is why this is referred to as the "Moriah Carry."

My apologies. This story is intense, and I needed a little break.

Isaac asked his father where the lamb for the offering was. Abraham replied,

> *"God himself will provide the lamb." —Genesis 22:8*

Abraham tied his son—the promise—to the altar. This was the boy he loved, fed, rocked, cared for, and played with. Isaac was old enough and strong enough to resist, but seemingly he did not.

> *[Abraham] reached out his hand and took the knife to slay his son. But the angel of the* Lord *called out to him from heaven, "Abraham! Abraham!"*
> *"Here I am," he replied. —Genesis 22:10–11*

Pause and imagine what those words sounded like coming out of Abraham's mouth: "Here I am." His elderly arm was in the air, shaking as he held the knife. Isaac's eyes were closed. Isaac didn't hear this plan directly from God, so he didn't understand what was going on, but he trusted his dad as much as Abraham trusted the Lord. Abraham's vision was blurred because his brain couldn't compute what was happening and his eyes couldn't see through the tears. Perhaps he said "Here I am" quietly because he was spent, worn out, exhausted. Perhaps he yelled the words because he was hoping, begging for God to stop him.

> *"Do not lay a hand on the boy," [God] said. "Do not do anything to him. Now I know that you fear God, because you have not withheld from me your son, your only son."*
> *—Genesis 22:12*

On the way up the mountain, Abraham told his son, "God will provide," which is mercifully what happened. They found a ram caught in a bush near them and sacrificed the ram instead of Isaac.

Who's Responsible?

Why the ram? Why did any blood have to be shed?

Through the ancient practice of sacrifice, guilt and blame were transferred from humans to something of value. Abraham and his family made some mistakes; they did some things wrong just as we all do. The idea is that all those mistakes were transferred to the ram, and the ram would die so Abraham and his family wouldn't have to.

This still sounds odd, but our modern experience is certainly familiar with the idea of clarifying who is to blame. When something goes wrong, we're quick to ask, "Who's responsible?" When significant revenue is lost at work, we don't just say, "Oh well, we'll make it up next quarter." We need to identify who's responsible. Somebody needs to pay. When we're involved in a car accident, we rarely get out of the vehicle and say, "I know I wasn't at fault, and I didn't see any errors on your end. I wonder what happened?" We want to point fingers. The police are about to arrive, and the insurance companies need to know who's responsible. Somebody must pay.

We rarely blame everybody equally because that's not satisfying. We rarely say, "Don't worry about it" and let it go, because we have an innate need for justice. And we rarely blame ourselves because we prefer to avoid consequences.

So we transfer blame. We seek out a sacrificial lamb. A scapegoat. Because somebody must pay.

Maybe this barbaric system of sacrifice is not completely archaic.

Connected

Abraham proved his faithfulness through his willingness to sacrifice his son. Imagine how different the story would have been if the angel had not stopped him. Could you imagine a father sacrificing his own son because he believed it was the best thing to do?

Could you imagine?

Isaac grew up and had children who had children. His grandson, Joseph, was sold into slavery by his jealous brothers. He was carted off to Egypt, which was about 450 miles away.

In Egypt, the family grew into a great nation and was freed from slavery by Moses. They wandered in the desert for forty years before entering the Promised Land.

Years later, David became king, conquered Jerusalem, and declared it the capital city of the nation.

The people of God ignored the numerous prophets who warned them they would get kicked out of this precious land if they continued to ignore the main character in the story. They didn't heed the warning, so they were scattered throughout the neighboring nations.

Eventually, some of them stumbled back to Jerusalem, which was now occupied by foreigners.

Centuries later, Jesus was born in Bethlehem. He grew up in a region called Galilee, eighty-five miles north of Jerusalem. Jesus was tried as a criminal and crucified on a cross on a mountain. Do you know how far that mountain was from Mount Moriah where Abraham almost sacrificed his son?

Five hundred yards.

From the spot where Abraham's son was nearly sacrificed to the cross where God's Son *was* sacrificed....

Five hundred yards.

This is the setting of the story. It's known as the "Fertile Crescent," the Promised Land, and is where the modern-day nation of Israel is located. It's the Holy Land. It's the now-active city built on a piece of dirt that has seen some of the most significant moments in human history. These pieces are connected.

When John the Baptist first saw Jesus, he said,

> *"Look, the Lamb of God, who takes away the sin of the world!"*
> *—John 1:29*

We read these words and it's possible they have very little meaning for us. We don't sacrifice animals. We don't transfer blame onto a perfect lamb so that our sins can be taken away. We may not think much about old Abraham, who almost sacrificed his own son.

But these stories are connected. When God laid the foundation of the earth, he had a plan. He wasn't making this story up as he went along. He didn't have a "Plan A" that was the Old Testament and then, when it failed, move on to "Plan B" in the New Testament.

Sometimes the two-by-four directly in front of us looks terrific. There's a beautiful story that warms the heart. There's a fascinating discovery that stimulates the mind. There's a verse in the Bible that rings true and is worthy of being memorized or framed and hung on the wall. There's a story from the Scriptures that makes sense and has stood the test of time. We're thankful for those pieces of wood, and we want to experience a whole pile of lumber like that. We want to form a structure out of only those pieces of wood. We can put our faith in a God like that.

But sometimes we experience lumber that seems rotten, twisted, and ugly. We discover something about God's creation that doesn't make sense to us. We come across a verse that we wish was not in the Bible. We read a story about a God who commanded a man to sacrifice his son, and we're not endeared to that God.

When you come across an ugly two-by-four, don't assume the whole structure is unsightly. Not every piece of wood is beautiful, but they're all connected. It's *one* story that began in *one* corner of the world, where God started with *one* nation.

1. From *Star Wars: The Force Awakens*. I believe the Bible is all true; it is supernaturally inspired, preserved across time, cultures, and continents, delivered to us, useful for reproof and instruction, and for righteousness. The Scriptures are our backstop, the ultimate field of inquiry and judgment, the measure of conduct, faith, and practice. All other sources of knowledge fall beneath their shadow. At the same time, I also believe there's room at the table for dialogue about the "nuts and bolts" of it all. It's imperative that we understand the overarching narrative of the Old Testament and value its place in the story before we dissect the details.

1.3 Children of God

My kids grew up watching Dora the Explorer. They liked her because she was happy, adventurous, and easy to understand. If puzzles were rated on a difficulty scale of one to ten, Dora was dealing with challenges that would rate about minus two. The kids enjoyed it, but it was not very stimulating for us parents.

One of the riveting characters on the show was The Map, and whenever it was introduced in an episode it would sing its theme song: "I'm The Map, I'm The Map, I'm The Map, I'm The Map—*I'm The Map!*"

If you're familiar with the show, you likely cringed when you read those words and heard the tune in your head. If you're not familiar with the show, you're likely unimpressed with the creativity of the lyrics.

But Dora the Explorer was not written for you and me; it was written for preschoolers. We must speak differently when we're speaking to children. We must avoid subtlety and sarcasm and obscure references. We must approach everything in a way that relates to and connects with them.

The grand narrative of human existence is a love story between God and his people. God laid the foundation of that relationship through a family that became one nation. But that nation had no concept of what was expected of them and no sense of right or wrong. In the first half of the Old Testament, God had to treat this young nation like children. He had to approach everything in a way that related to and connected with them.

Start With Trust, Not Love

The goal of the story is love. God (the first character) demonstrated his love for us (the second character) repeatedly throughout the story and ultimately through the sacrifice of his Son on the cross—a story we will explore in the New Testament.[1] God's design is for us to return that love, and it must be returned willingly. We must have the freedom to choose whether we love God back.

At this point in the story, however, the Israelites were still children. They did not yet have the maturity to love God back.

Children don't have the capacity to give mature love. They need love and they receive it well, but they're not capable of unconditional or sacrificial love. They don't think, "I should probably stop screaming in the restaurant because everyone seems to be looking, and it must be horribly embarrassing for my mom and dad." They're not ready to love, but they are ready to trust. The parent loves the child so the child will learn to trust the parent, which is the precursor to love.

Let's return to the Israelites. They were in slavery in Egypt and grew in strength and number. God chose Moses to free them from slavery in a dramatic story of plagues and miracles. After crossing the Red Sea, they wandered in the desert in search of the fertile land God had promised them. These "children of God" were hungry and thirsty and wondering if they should have trusted Moses and his God:

> *"If only we had died by the LORD's hand in Egypt! There we sat around pots of meat and ate all the food we wanted, but you have brought us out into this desert to starve this entire assembly to death." —Exodus 16:3*

To which God responded,

> *"I will rain down bread from heaven for you. The people are to go out each day and gather enough for that day. In this way I will test them and see whether they will follow my instructions." —Exodus 16:4*

The bread was called *manna*, which means, "What is it?" They looked at the stuff, knowing it was from God, but didn't know what it was. Parents, when your kids look at the food you have provided and they ask, "What is it?" in an unappreciative way, you can now take it as a compliment, because they are referring to it as manna from heaven.

Each morning, the people were to collect the manna they needed for that day—nothing more, nothing less. God wanted his children to understand they could trust him every day. God was saying, "I see you, I hear you, I know you're struggling—but I want you to trust me one step at a time." Thousands of years later, Jesus modeled for us how to pray:

> *"[Father,] give us this day our daily bread."*
> *—Matthew 6:11 (King James Version)*

This day, our *daily* bread. One day at a time.

In the desert, God was preparing his children. In the next chapter of this book, we will see how they would become a mighty nation with great wealth and power. They would be asked to do things they didn't want to do. They would be asked to give up things they didn't want to release. Before all that happened, could they begin the early stages of love? Could they trust God one day at a time, one moment at a time?

God had to start somewhere.

Start with Boundaries, Not Freedom

The goal was also freedom. Later in the story, we discover with clarity that Jesus came to set us free. Free to choose, free to wait, free to walk away, free to surrender all. But when caregivers are developing children, they don't start with freedom; they start with boundaries. They don't let six-year-olds fill the grocery basket with whatever they want. They provide them with guidelines and prepare them for their future freedom.

My wife, Tami, and I watched *Supersize Me* when our kids were little, and we stopped our weekly routine of enjoying McDonald's. We weren't wholly sensible because we switched to Wendy's instead. Baby steps, I guess.

But we *were* consistent regarding soda. We essentially removed it from our home and told our kids they couldn't drink it. It was a firm boundary, and the kids didn't know what they were missing, so it was very manageable. At age five, our oldest asked us when he would be able to drink the forbidden beverage. We hadn't discussed an age, so I just picked one that seemed forever away.

"Ten. You can drink soda when you're ten."

The boundary was set, and it was terrific. On his tenth birthday, we celebrated with a "pop party." As I recall, he spoke very rapidly that day and acted like a scavenging squirrel. It was part of his growth from boundaries to freedom. He was learning that it's okay to trust a loving authority to set reasonable limitations.

The ancient nation of Israel was on a growth plan as well. They were set free from the physical boundaries of slavery in Egypt, but they were not yet ready for *freedom* as we understand and revere it today. They were still *children*, and they needed numerous boundaries and rules.

The Law

Strap a two-year-old in a car seat and you're likely to see evidence that humans don't like boundaries. We don't like restrictions and we don't like to be told what we can and can't do. Many view religion as a system that enforces a litany of archaic, indisputable laws.

More accurately, we don't like laws that limit *me*. The existence and enforcement of laws is rather interesting to most of us, as evidenced by the popularity of courtroom dramas on television and in movies. In the real world, we're huge fans of laws that protect *us*. We're thankful for an organized society that protects the rights and property of its citizens.

But where did these laws come from? We think they're innate—that we are born with a general sense of human decency and that all people should be treated with dignity and respect. But we don't come home from the hospital nursery with those values. Look at the actions and responses of toddlers playing on a playground: they want what they want and, left to themselves, they're unconcerned about the effect of their actions on others.

The newly formed nation of Israel was a group of spiritual and moral children. If a man wanted another man's wife, he would kill that man and take his wife. Why not? If a man wanted sons to continue his bloodline, but his wife was barren, he would take another wife or sleep with his wife's maid. Why not? They didn't have any boundaries to tell them otherwise.

So God provided his children with a foundational set of rules: the Ten Commandments (found in Exodus 20). The first five address the relationship between God and us.

1. ***You shall have no other gods before me.*** This command is about trusting God above all other things and all other people. Few of us have three or four religious beings we are singing about and praying to. But we have hobbies, sports, work, and even family relationships that, at times, occupy the top spot. There's nothing wrong with enjoying these things; it's an issue of priority.

2. ***You shall not make for yourself an image (idol).*** The immature Israelites formed a golden calf once while they were waiting for Moses to return. They danced and partied around that calf as a substitute for God. The idea here is that there is no substitute for God. God is not *in* an item. He's not an essence that is distributed throughout his creation. God is a loving, thinking, communicating being. He's the main character in the story.

3. ***You shall not misuse the name of the Lord your God.*** I cringe when people use the name "God" or "Jesus" as a curse word because I really like God and I have a relationship with him. I would feel much the same if people used my wife's name in a similar manner. The third commandment, however, is addressing more than that concern. This law is about putting God's name on thoughts and ideas that did not come from him. It's a caution about using phrases such as "God told me..." or "God wants you to...." Let God speak for himself, and don't misuse his name.

4. ***Remember the Sabbath day by keeping it holy.*** The seventh day of creation was a day of rest; one of our days should be as well. This is not a suggestion. It's not like flossing your teeth or drinking eight cups of water a day. This made it on God's "top-ten list" to his developing children.

5. ***Honor your father and your mother.*** Again, the goal is for us to trust and eventually love God. Our relationship with God starts with our parents because we see their faces and we can't yet conceive of an omniscient, spiritual being. We honor father and mother first, and as we mature, it is hoped that honor will transfer to God.

The second half of the list shifts from our relationship with God to our relationships with others. Each of these five commandments is about protecting something as a powerful way of loving and honoring others.

6. *You shall not murder.* The sixth commandment is about protecting the most valuable set of molecules in the universe: human life. In all shapes, colors, and sizes, every imperfect, broken and mistreated life must be protected.
7. *You shall not commit adultery.* This is about protecting the family unit as the backbone of a healthy and thriving society. When marriage is devalued, kids suffer. When kids suffer, the future is marred. There are tremendous consequences to those secret, playful relationships at work.
8. *You shall not steal.* It may surprise you to learn that God values your stuff. This commandment is about protecting what you own because God highly values the owner.
9. *You shall not give false testimony against your neighbor.* The modern judicial system was based on these ten ancient laws. If we can't trust what people are saying, then we won't have access to the truth. This commandment protects something incredibly valuable to each of us: our reputation. It doesn't protect us from ruining our own reputation; it protects us from being tainted by a false testimony.
10. *You shall not covet.* This final boundary is essentially about protecting everything else. You have what you have. Enjoy it and don't be distracted by what others have.

A New Command

The Ten Commandments are an amazing list of ideas that have had an immeasurable impact on subsequent and modern civilizations. They were carved in stone more than three thousand years ago for a lawless group of people who were the focus of God's attention. They were written as a guide for the children of God who were generations away from spiritual and moral maturity.

They still have application to our lives, but they were not written for us.

Keep reading, and I will explain.

Don't get me wrong. I don't mean that the Ten Commandments are irrelevant to us or that we get to dismiss them. They remain the moral bedrock of human existence; their truth transcends cultures, continents, and millennia.

You and I can read the Ten Commandments, research them, memorize them, and be affected by them. But they weren't written for us. They were words given by God as he was parenting his children. He gave them what they needed at that time. The same can and should be said about all the other laws found in the Old Testament. They were given to a different group of people at a different developmental stage.

When we get confused by the huge pile of moral two-by-fours in our lives, we are wise to revisit foundational ideas such as the Ten Commandments. But in the grand story, much has been built on top of them.

When my son Martin was little, he often talked with his mouth full. He was as excited about the food he was eating as he was about the story he was telling, so he didn't have the ability to pause either one. I would point my finger to my mouth and say to him, "Don't talk with your mouth full. I don't want to see your food. I don't want to hear the sloshing, slapping sound of the food in your mouth." He didn't understand. He was offended. He didn't like the rule and needed me to repeat it about six times per meal.

Fast-forward fifteen years. I'm the same dad and he's the same son. I still have the same boundaries about seeing and hearing partially chewed food at the dinner table. The message, however, is different because he's at a very different developmental stage. Those old dinner-table rules still apply, but I am no longer required to verbalize them, and we can talk about new things.

God is still the main character, but you and I have a relationship with him that falls much later in the Overall story. As upcoming chapters will show, there are many changes throughout the biblical narrative.

In Part III, we will see how Jesus addressed these old laws on multiple occasions. He summarized them and boiled them down to a "new command."[2] He didn't erase the Ten Commandments—he simply offered a newer and more mature message around the dinner table.

1. Romans 5:8.
2. John 13:34–35.

1.4 You Are That Person

"We want a king...we want a king...we want a king!"

This chant could be heard throughout the mighty nation of Israel. God's plan was that *he* would be their king. This is called a *theocracy*, but the children of God thought it was *theo-crazy*. They wanted to have a human king just like all the other nations around them.

"We want a king...we want a king...we want a king!"

Let me back up a little. After forty years wandering in the desert, the Israelites came to the Promised Land (where modern-day Israel is located, plus parts of surrounding countries). Led by Joshua, they took possession of the area one city at a time. God's unique political plan was to be their king and provide regional leaders (called *judges*) when needed. For over three hundred years, there was a repeated pattern:

- The people would forget about God.
- A neighboring nation would oppress them.
- God would raise up a leader/judge who would defeat the enemy.
- Peace would be restored.

Eventually, the people called for political reform: "We want a king... we want a king...we want a king!"

A prophet was a spiritual leader who spoke to the people on behalf of God. God chose to provide his people with their desired king, and he used a prophet named Samuel to select that king. The first selection was a man named Saul. Saul was an impressive individual who stood a head taller than anyone else.[1] But sadly, his character couldn't keep up with his stature and he did not thrive as king.

God then instructed Samuel to choose Israel's next king.

David

David was the youngest and smallest of the eight boys in his family. His selection as king was a surprise to his brothers, to his dad, and to Samuel himself.

"Are you sure? The little one with the acne problem?"

> *"The LORD does not look at the things people look at. People look at the outward appearance, but the LORD looks at the heart." —1 Samuel 16:7*

This chapter is about King David, the greatest king in Israel's storied history. Selection day had to be terrific for David as he looked at the faces of his seven jealous brothers. Soon after that, he whapped Goliath with a stone from his slingshot, then he used the giant's sword to remove his head. We rarely add that last "Hollywood-esque" detail, but it's in there. Good times.

The story didn't continue smoothly for David, however. King Saul had raging jealousy toward this young man. He asked David to come and play his harp to calm him down, but then he would snap and throw spears at David. It didn't seem that the soothing sound of the harp was doing its job. David had to run and hide from Saul. At one point, he wanted to escape to a nearby town, but he knew they would recognize him as the famous giant-killer, so he pretended to be a madman, scratching on doors and drooling down his beard.[2] Less-good times.

David persevered and became a courageous and powerful king. The only city in the Promised Land that the Israelites had not been able to overtake was the well-fortified city of Jebus. David discovered a way in, conquered the Jebusites, and renamed the city *Jerusalem*. Since then, the piece of land has also been known as the City of David.

David was also a prolific songwriter; he is credited with nearly half the songs in the 150 chapters of the Book of Psalms. Personally, I struggle with David's songs because so many of them are complaints:

> *My God, my God, why have you forsaken me? —Psalm 22:1*

> *Why, LORD, do you reject me and hide your face from me? —Psalm 88:14*

All day long my enemies taunt me.... I eat ashes as my food and mingle my drink with tears. —Psalm 102:8–9

I used to think David was a whiner.

No—he was a leader.

It took me years to realize the loneliness and isolation of leadership. David worked hard to become a great king. He was committed to his calling and inspired passion among his people. And through it all, he had countless naysayers, challenges, and opposition. He wasn't a complainer; he was an experienced leader.

But he wasn't perfect.

Bathsheba

One evening, during the peak of his kingship, David walked around on the rooftop of his palace and saw a woman bathing. We men are so simple. And so stupid.

It's the classic story. Boy meets girl; girl is married to a soldier under boy's command; boy gets girl pregnant; soldier refuses to leave his post and be with girl; boy sends soldier to die in battle; boy gets girl. I think it's obvious why Disney has not yet made an animated version.

David's actions in this story have sadly reverberated through millennia. He was a man of influence who used his outrageous power to manipulate a woman who was unable to resist. Our natural tendency is to separate ourselves from the story of David and Bathsheba because we have not done anything so appalling. That's *David's* story, not mine.

The last five of the Ten Commandments are about protecting things. When we break these laws, we are taking something that does not belong to us. We all have our own version of a Bathsheba. Every one of us has taken opportunities to damage someone else's reputation. All parents have wounded their kids by words said and decisions made. Every husband has hidden something from his wife, and every wife has dreamed of a life she doesn't have.

I went through David's story quickly because I want to focus less on what he did and more on how he responded. Initially, David wanted to get away with it and enjoy his new wife and child, but he had a pesky friend named Nathan who told him a fictional story about two men. One was wealthy and had numerous sheep; the other was poor and had one little lamb that he cared for like a daughter. In preparation for a meal, the rich man took the little lamb from the poor man instead of choosing any of his own numerous sheep.

David was outraged. He wanted to use his kingly power to ensure justice against this wretched man from Nathan's story. The wealthy and powerful must *not* be allowed to take advantage of the weak and the poor. Not in my kingdom!

Then Nathan said to David, "You are that man."

Nathans are very rare. Few of us have people in our lives who care about us enough and are bold enough to say such things. Few of us have a Nathan; all of us need one.

Two Versions

There are two versions of the story of David in God's Word. There's the *Samuel* version that comes first and is the one we've been looking at in this chapter. Then the entire story of David and the other kings is retold in the *Chronicles* version. Two versions, back-to-back. But the story of Bathsheba is curiously missing from the Chronicles version, as is any mention of other mistakes David made. The Chronicles version is like a résumé. It shows all the great things David did and how perfect he would be if one were looking to hire a king.

Honesty and authenticity are cherished in our culture. We don't want our heroes to be perfect; we want them to be real. We connect with imperfection because we see it in the mirror. There is, however, a time for the *Chronicles* version of our story. We don't have to dump our laundry onto every person we meet. When the cashier at Chick-fil-A asks how you're doing, she's not prepared to hear the details of your upcoming divorce.

There's a time for the Chronicles version, but most of us don't even *have* a *Samuel* version of our story. We want authenticity from others, but are we willing to give it? Have you ever shared your weaknesses, mistakes, and blemishes with others? Are you growing and developing through the *Samuel* version of your story, or are you protecting it by pointing fingers at others? "At least I'm not like so-and-so, who did that. At least I didn't have an affair. At least I didn't have her husband killed." We claw for innocence-by-comparison.

Villains

Who would you say is the most horrific villain in any story you have ever read, heard, or seen? Think of a moment when a character did something so heinous that you wanted to dive into the book, or jump at the screen, and stop it from happening. A moment in a story that makes you squirm right now as you think about it. There's something inside you that screams, "You can't do that!" Maybe it's the warden from *Shawshank Redemption* or the stepmother in *Cinderella* or Javert from *Les Misérables*. For me, the most disturbing villain is Hannibal Lecter.[3] That guy is messed up. He's calm, brilliant, manipulative, and scary. We get stirred up by villains because the innocent must be protected. It's not right for the wealthy and the powerful to take advantage of the poor and the weak.

When you think of that heinous villain and you feel that rage inside, imagine Nathan looking at you, with love and compassion in his eyes. And he whispers, "You are that person." Whatever evil we can imagine from one human to another, that is the weight of our indiscretions. It's natural for us to be horrified by the actions of others and downplay our own, but any selfish or unhealthy pain we cause others is abhorrent to our Creator.

"You are that person."

Remember, the primary goal of the Overall story is for the second character (us) to be madly in love with the first character (God). God's love for us is a given. It was there from the very beginning, and it will not waver. Our love for God, however, is something that can grow and develop throughout the story. And every journey, every pathway, every story that goes from "I don't know who God is" to "I love God wholeheartedly" goes through brokenness. Every one.

We celebrate stories of extraordinary transformation. Men who leave their families and pursue every conceivable selfish desire, then come back home and beg for a second chance because God has done a miracle in their hearts. Women who plummet into a pit of depression and alcoholism, then surrender their lives to God and crawl out one arduous step at a time. We love these stories. I *know* these stories. I know people who have experienced these incredible things.

But this is *all* our stories. Every pathway back to God goes through brokenness. To experience restoration, we must acknowledge our depravity. You are that person, and you need the same forgiveness and the same restoration as the most heinous villains you could imagine.

Full Restoration

Before we move on, it's important to step back and look at the big picture. We now have a few two-by-fours on the pile. We have a basic idea of the overall relationship between the three main characters, and we see how God laid the foundation with the ancient nation of Israel.

As we look at the lumber from this chapter—the story of King David—why is there a need for Jesus later in the story? If we can break the laws of God as blatantly as David did, then respond well as David did and be restored as king, then why would there ever be a need for Jesus? If we can mess up, seek forgiveness, then be restored—all without Jesus—then why do we need the other parts of the story?

The narrative answer is that David was not fully restored. His peak preceded his mistake with Bathsheba. He was challenged by Nathan and responded well. You can find his "journal entry" from this event in Psalm 51. But he never fully recovered. Bathsheba gave birth to a son who became ill and died. One of David's daughters was raped by her half-brother who was then killed by another son of David. A different son betrayed his father and forced David out of the great city that was his namesake. David survived and he remained king, but he suffered significant consequences.

The theological answer will take shape over the next few chapters. The central and most spectacular part of the Overall story is Jesus, but the way to fully appreciate him is to understand these broken moments that lead to him.

So stay with me, one beautifully imperfect piece of lumber at a time.

---

1. 1 Samuel 9:2.
2. 1 Samuel 21:13.
3. This fictional character was created by novelist Thomas Harris, but he was made famous by the 1991 film *The Silence of the Lambs*.

1.5 What...Is Your Quest?

Bob and Ziggy Marley. Kirk and Michael Douglas. Dick and Rick Hoyt (Team Hoyt). Pierre and Justin Trudeau. Marlin and Nemo. Gordie and Mark Howe. Bobby and Barry Bonds. Anakin and Luke Skywalker. Homer and Bart Simpson.

There have been numerous remarkable father-son teams, but none have had a greater impact on human history than David and Solomon (deities excluded, of course).

David and Bathsheba's love child did not survive more than seven days, but they later had a son named Solomon, whose name comes from the word *shalom*, which means "peace and harmony." David was a man of war; Solomon was a man of peace. Solomon is the last great two-by-four we'll explore in Part I, the origin story of the ancient nation of Israel. He reigned for forty years as king, and it was a time of tremendous growth, prosperity, and harmony.

Solomon's first task was to build the great temple in Jerusalem. It was a magnificent structure that symbolized the wealth and power of the Israelite kingdom. Soon after, God appeared to Solomon in a dream and made him an incredible offer:

> *"Ask for whatever you want me to give you." —1 Kings 3:5*

I asked my seven-year-old son what he would do if God entered his room and made this offer.

"I would do nothing."

Why?

"Because I would faint if God actually entered my room."

Fair enough.

How would *you* respond? Solomon asked for wisdom—more

accurately, a "discerning heart"—and we'll look at that in a moment. But Solomon's response was not *the* response. It was not the only right answer. The relationship between the first character and second character is beautifully unique for each person, and each of us has the freedom to respond in our own way.

Some of you read the title of this chapter and knew the reference immediately. You are my people. Others will learn right now that the title is a line from *Monty Python and the Holy Grail*, and you are rolling your eyes at the absurdity of people who love that movie. I have served as a pastor for many years, and I have used numerous clips from *The Holy Grail*. Each time, I looked forward to the moment and was disappointed when only a few people seemed to share my enthusiasm. My loving wife always says, "When will you learn not to use anything from that movie?" Perhaps I need more of a discerning heart.

Until then, my zeal remains. Maybe this will be the reference that finally connects....

King Arthur and his dwindling crew encountered a troll at a bridge. To pass, they had to answer three questions. First was, "What...is your name?" Most of us can handle that one easily (although there are times in life when even this one is difficult—times when we don't even know who we are). The second question was, "What...is your quest?" and it's the focus of this chapter. I will skip the third question and encourage you to enjoy it in the context of the movie.

What...is your quest? As you look at your plans for the next year, as you think about your hopes, your dreams, and what you want to accomplish, as you reflect on why you're even reading this book—what do you seek? What do you *really* want? It's a profound question that Jesus will ask later on in the Overall story.[1] Go beyond the answer that is expected of you or the answer you feel you are *supposed* to give. What are you truly longing for in life? Be honest.

Is it purpose? influence? fame? power? peace? love?

On the front cover, and on the first page of each of the seven parts in this book, there's a diagram that looks like this:

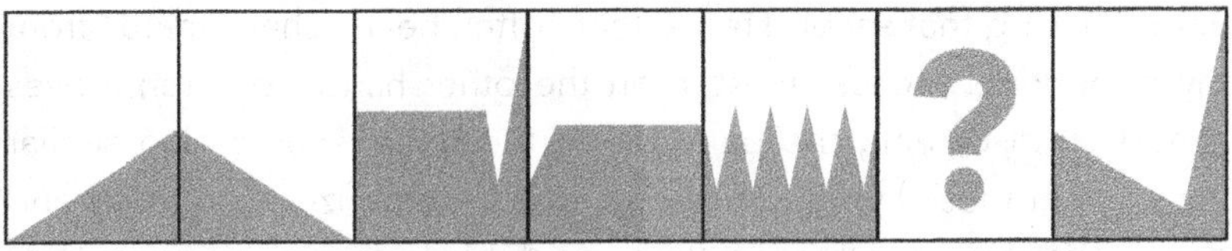

It's divided into the seven parts of the story. The x-axis is time. It represents movement from the very beginning of the story, through the seven parts, to the end of life as we know it. The y-axis essentially represents how well things are going in each part of the story. The graph is steadily rising during the first half of the Old Testament because it's the story of the Israelite nation's growth and development. Then the graph steadily descends during Part II, which is the next section. After that, it bounces around quite a bit over the next five parts.

If you could label the y-axis, what would you call it? What does it mean for life to go well or not to go well? If moving up on the y-axis means that life is good, how would you label it? Perhaps it would be helpful to call it the *why-axis*. Why do you get up in the morning? Why do you work so hard? Why do you want next year to be better than this year?

What...is your quest? What do you seek? Allow your answer to that question to shape you as you continue building the framework of the Overall story.

A Discerning Heart

In Solomon's response to God's offer, he said,

> *"I am only a little child and do not know how to carry out my duties." —1 Kings 3:7*

Solomon's self-aware comment reflected the young nation of Israel as a whole. They were children in need of guidance and direction. Solomon then asked for a "discerning heart."

Discernment is the ability to see things before they happen. This is possible because humans are rather predictable. When person *A* is faced with circumstances *B* and *C*, there's a good chance the outcome will be *D*. Wisdom is the ability to see these patterns. When I play chess, I can see typically two moves ahead. It's when I get excited about making that second move that I often hear "Check mate" from my opponent. A chess master, on the other hand, sees ten moves ahead by discerning the patterns on the board. Something similar happens in music. Great musicians don't memorize every note and chord. They become fluent in the predictable language of music. They discover the consistent patterns.

Wise people see the patterns in life. They see what happens when you spend significant, intimate time with someone who is not your spouse. They see what happens after an evening that goes beyond two glasses of wine. They see what happens with young girls whose dads are trapped in an addiction. Wise people see patterns and respond to them without assuming they are the exception.

Solomon was one of the wisest persons to have ever lived. He could see the next ten moves for everyone else's pieces on the chess board. But he was awful at managing his own piece on the board. He was not able to see the pattern of what happens when you pursue multiple forbidden women from neighboring nations. He collected seven hundred of them as wives, as well as three hundred as concubines. Our ability to *not* see destructive patterns in our own lives is astounding.

Path...to the Quest

There are two kinds of people: those who believe we can't divide the world into two kinds of people, and those who believe we can.

I happen to be the latter. There are Psalms-people and there are Proverbs-people. The Book of Psalms was written primarily by David, whereas the Book of Proverbs is attributed to his son Solomon. Psalms-people are right-brained creatives who love the honesty and poetry of the ancient songs. Proverbs-people are left-brained thinkers who love the logic and reason of the ancient writings.

It's not about choosing one or the other. Poets will always benefit from reason and structure, while thinkers will always be stretched by passion and creativity. But most of us have a natural leaning. If you're unsure of yours, try a little exercise with me. Interlock your fingers in front of you like you're an obedient child in elementary school. Your thumbs should be resting on top of each other. If your right thumb is on top, you're likely a Psalms-person. If your left thumb is on top, you're likely a Proverbs-person. How's that for scientific accuracy?

I'm a left-thumb, Proverbs-person (with an odd bent toward creativity). The older I get, the more I understand and appreciate the Psalms, but I have always gravitated toward the short, pithy wisdom of Proverbs. In chapter three, the wisest man in the world wrote this:

> *Trust in the Lord with all your heart*
> *and lean not on your own understanding;*
> *in all your ways submit to him,*
> *and he will make your paths straight.* —Proverbs 3:5–6

There are two possible paths. One is marked "Trust in the Lord." It's the path that leads to whatever we identify as the *why-axis* on the graph of growth and development. It's what we truly seek deep in our bones: purpose, love, peace, joy. It is our quest.

The other path is marked "Your Own Understanding." We tend to choose this second path for several reasons. Perhaps we don't *believe* the first character in the story exists or has our best interests in mind. How can I trust God with my quest? The only person I can truly trust is myself. I will make it happen. I will overcome any obstacles along the way. Or perhaps we don't *know* about the first path. We're not choosing the second path over the first path—we simply don't know that a "Trust in the Lord" path exists. Or, thirdly, some of us don't *care*. We know exactly what God is asking us to do or not do. We know exactly what it means to take the "Trust in the Lord" path and that it will lead us to our deep-rooted quest. But we want what we want. We desire something down the second path, and we pursue it, no matter the cost.

> Two possible paths.
>
> Two roads diverged in a wood, and I—
>
> I took the one less traveled by,
>
> And that has made all the difference.[2]

The great news is that it's never too late to choose the "Trust in the Lord" path. There are multiple trails that allow that to happen. No matter how far we are down the "Your Own Understanding" path, there's a trail that cuts back to the God path.

The presence of these trails that return us to the "Trust in the Lord" path demonstrates God's love and mercy, but they are not without risk. Some who are faithful to God may think, "I'm bored with being good. I want a *past*. I want a testimony that will impress middle-schoolers and make Gramma blush." If you seek a relationship with God, why risk getting lost on the wrong path? Loving parents make great efforts to protect their kids from making foolish decisions. Yes, they can be restored. Yes, they can recover. But there is so much at stake. Some risks are adventurous, others are unwise.

Meaningless!

What…is your quest?

As wise as Solomon was, he never really figured this out for himself. As a new king, he started well, but then he drifted. The Book of Ecclesiastes is historically credited to Solomon and was likely written later in his life. It's an abrasive challenge to the predictable patterns of human nature. It has been said that those under forty years old shouldn't even read the book because it's sad and demented. But those over forty read it and think, "That's what I thought!"

The book begins rather boldly:

> *"Utterly meaningless! Everything is meaningless."*
> *—Ecclesiastes 1:2*

This is a verse people rarely hang on their walls. With refreshing honesty, Solomon reflected on some of the quests he had pursued in his life:

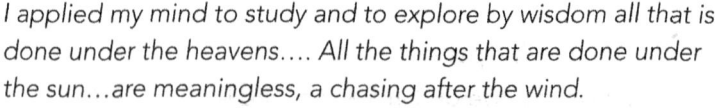

> *I applied my mind to study and to explore by wisdom all that is done under the heavens…. All the things that are done under the sun…are meaningless, a chasing after the wind.*
> *—Ecclesiastes 1:13–14*

> *I said to myself, "Come now, I will test you with pleasure to find out what is good." But that also proved to be meaningless.*
> *—Ecclesiastes 2:1*

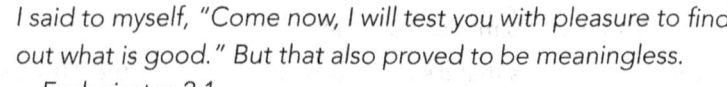

> *I hated all the things I had toiled for under the sun, because I must leave them to the one who comes after me. And who knows whether that person will be wise or foolish? Yet they will have control over all the fruit of my toil into which I have poured my effort and skill under the sun. This too is meaningless. —Ecclesiastes 2:18–19*

Can you recall a quest in your life that was of utmost importance but now seems meaningless? Can you imagine your future self viewing some of your current quests as a chasing after the wind? Before we head into the next part of the story, what do you seek in life? What shapes your decisions? What determines good days from not-so-good days?

What...is your quest?

1. John 1:37–38.
2. Robert Frost, "The Road Not Taken."

PART II: VIOLATION

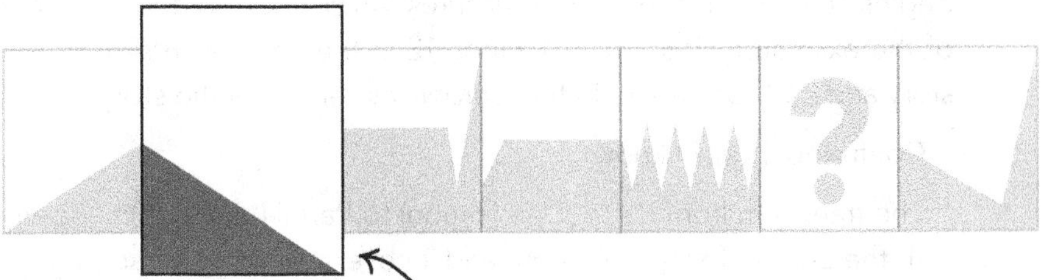

Violation: the decline of God's people, leading to the exile

Intro

"Let me tell you why you're here. You're here because you know something. What you know you can't explain, but you feel it. Do you know what I'm talking about?"

"The exile."

"Do you want to know what it is?"[1]

The exile is the greatest Bible story you've never heard of. It's the central story for forty-one percent of the Old Testament and thirty-one percent of the entire Bible.[2] Yet most who identify themselves as *Christian* are shockingly unfamiliar with the story. I graduated with a master's degree in theology and could not have told you the story of the exile. In Part II, we find some of the most challenging books in the Bible to read. They are often long and difficult to understand. Our goal is to turn some lumber into framework so that we can learn from this essential part of the Overall story.

Even those with very little church experience are familiar with the classics:

- Noah and the ark
- Moses and the parting of the Red Sea
- David and Goliath

But I'm not aware of an animated film about the exile, or a company that provides items to decorate a child's room with an *exile* theme.

Part II is a story of violation. God's people ignored his laws and boundaries, and God chose to respond. It's the tragic story of the fall of ancient Israel and it's the grand setup for the coming of Jesus. It begins at an odd place in the Scriptures, which is part of the obscurity of the exile story. It starts in 1 Kings 12 in the *Samuel* version of the story and 2 Chronicles 10 in the *Chronicles* version of the story.[3]

Confusing, right? I know.

The transition from Part I (One Nation) to Part II (Violation) happens with the death of King Solomon, and it covers the story of Israel drifting further and further away from the God who created them and provided for them.

In Part II we find the *prophets* of the Old Testament, and nearly every one was warning the people before the exile, comforting them during the exile, or providing hope beyond the exile.

Essentially, God's people had now developed into *teenagers*. They were not kids anymore, and God had to parent and lead them differently.

---

1. This is a slightly adjusted version of a pivotal exchange between Neo and Morpheus from the 1999 movie *The Matrix*.
2. Based on the percentage of pages. In a sample 1,140-page Bible with no commentary or extra writings, Part I covers 512 pages and Part II covers 357.
3. These *versions* were mentioned in Chapter 1.4.

2.1 Division

The brain of a teenager is not fully developed.

When I was sixteen, I purchased my first car: a 1976 Pontiac Ventura. It was a tri-tone vehicle with a blue roof, a white body, and a six-inch reddish-brown racing stripe along the bottom (a.k.a. rust). I paid $425 for this beautiful symbol of freedom and wisely paid more than that for the stereo I installed in it.

While driving in a parking lot, someone clipped my rear bumper. Unlike the modern plastic bumpers, mine was solid metal. About a foot-and-a-half of it was bent back at a forty-five-degree angle. A sensible adult would have repaired or replaced it, but I was a teenager.

I loaded the car up with my friends on a Friday night, found a secluded telephone pole, aligned my vehicle about twenty feet away so that my rear bumper would make first contact, put the car in reverse, and stomped on the gas.

I discovered that a bent bumper on a 1976 Pontiac requires a tremendous amount of force to straighten. I had to ram it into the pole six times, much to the delight of my car's occupants.

The brain of a teenager is not fully developed.

We all have stories from this stage of life, which is why parents of preteens wish the whole family could hibernate for five to seven years, then wake up when the kids are young adults. Teenagers have an awkward and occasionally dangerous mixture of power/freedom and an underdeveloped prefrontal cortex.

In the second half of the Old Testament story, God's strategy for the growth and development of his people changed. In Part I (One Nation), he provided rules and boundaries to his *children*. Here in Part II, he treats them like *teenagers* and gives them more freedom to make their own decisions and experience their own consequences.

Enter...the Prophets

As a concept, *exile* means getting kicked out. Adam and Eve were exiled from the garden of Eden after they ate the forbidden fruit. Modern refugees are in exile when they are forced to leave their countries of origin that are in turmoil.

Have you ever been displaced? Have you ever had to reestablish patterns of life away from home? Perhaps you can remember heading off to college and lying down in your new bed after the excitement wore off. Maybe you moved from your hometown to start a new life in a different city. It can be exciting, but it can also be very unsettling. If you're forced to transition against your will, it can be devastating.

After Solomon died, the nation of Israel divided into the North (called *Israel*) and the South (called *Judah*). This is already confusing because the North managed to keep the original *Israel* name. Their lawyers must have claimed copyright ownership.

The *why-axis* graph on the Intro page of Part II (Violation) shows a steady downhill slope through this part of the Overall story. The kings in both the North and the South did not do well over this three-hundred-year period. Every king is listed and evaluated in the Bible. The number of kings in the North who did well in the eyes of the Lord: zero. The number in the South was not much higher.

Enter...the prophets.

Most of the second half of the Old Testament is the writings of the prophets. For many, these are the most difficult books in the Bible to understand. They are typically the most pristine, unmarked, crisp pages in our Bibles.

A prophet was a messenger who spoke to the people on behalf of God—as opposed to priests, who spoke to God on behalf of the people. There are *major* prophets—Isaiah, Jeremiah, Ezekiel, and Daniel—as well as twelve *minor* prophets. The distinction is solely based on the length of their books in the Bible and has nothing to do with importance. In the prophetic writings, you'll discover extraordinary nuggets, but you may have to do some mining to find them.

The overall goal of the prophets was to redirect and refocus the immature *teenage* nation that was increasingly violating the laws of

God. If they didn't reconnect with God, they would be exiled. They would be kicked out of the Promised Land they had worked so hard to find and develop.

The exile happened in two waves. The first was the Assyrian exile in 722 BC when Samaria, the capital city of the North, was taken over by the Assyrians.[1] Thousands of Israelites were removed, while thousands of Assyrians settled in to take their place—and their wives. This inter-marrying led to an "impure" breed of Jewish people, which is why the Samaritans were despised later in the biblical story.

The second wave was the more widely known Babylonian exile, which occurred in 586 BC when the city of Jerusalem, including Solomon's temple, was burned to the ground and the people of Judah were taken away to Babylon.[2]

A basic understanding of the exile allows readers of the Old Testament prophets to ask a couple helpful questions:

- Was this prophet addressing the North, the South, both, or (in a few cases) neither?
- Was this prophet writing before, during, or after the exile?

These questions at least move us beyond the "I-have-no-idea-what's-going-on" initial reaction to the prophetic writings.

Divided Kingdom

The exile story begins with two men who were the leading candidates to succeed Solomon as king of Israel. Their names were Rehoboam and Jeroboam, which is unfortunate because the names sound so similar. This story must not be fabricated, because why would someone create a story where the two main characters have nearly identical names?

To help with this dilemma, Rehoboam (with an "R") was the *real* son of Solomon, whereas Jeroboam (with a "J") was *just* an advisor to Solomon. Rehoboam had positional power, while Jeroboam had influential power.

Solomon died, and Rehoboam became king. He was approached by the people, including Jeroboam, who said,

> *"Your father put a heavy yoke on us, but now lighten the harsh labor and the heavy yoke he put on us, and we will serve you."*
> *—1 Kings 12:4*

Rehoboam asked for a few days to consider his response. He first sought guidance from the nation's experienced elders, who advised him to be merciful. He then ran it by his young buddies, who suggested that he respond in a similar way to Hans and Franz from a 1980s Saturday Night Live skit:

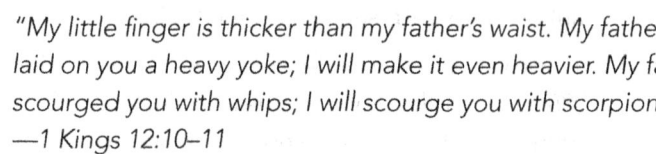

> *"My little finger is thicker than my father's waist. My father laid on you a heavy yoke; I will make it even heavier. My father scourged you with whips; I will scourge you with scorpions."*
> *—1 Kings 12:10–11*

They were there to pump (clap), him up.[3]

Guess which pathway Rehoboam chose? He was a new leader, and he responded like a teenager with new-found power. He wasn't interested in the wisdom and compassion of his elders because they "didn't know anything." The elders were stuck in the old world and didn't understand the *new* world like his cool friends did. As a result, the mighty nation of Israel split into the North (with Samaria as its capital and Jeroboam as its king) and the South (with Jerusalem as its capital and Rehoboam as its king).

Cannot Stand

You might be surprised at the number of widely used axioms that come directly from the Bible. In Part I (One Nation) alone, we have:

- "Scapegoat" (Leviticus 16:10)
- "Nothing but skin and bones" (Job 19:20)
- "I have escaped only by the skin of my teeth" (Job 19:20)
- "They were at their wits' end" (Psalm 107:27)
- "As iron sharpens iron, so one person sharpens another" (Proverbs 27:17)
- "There is nothing new under the sun" (Ecclesiastes 1:9)

Before his immortal *Gettysburg Address*, Abraham Lincoln accepted the nomination to be a United States senator with a famous speech that began, "A house divided against itself cannot stand."

He was addressing the growing tension between those who wanted to advocate for slavery and those who wanted to abolish it. Many credit Lincoln with this famous saying, but he was quoting Jesus, who was responding to those who were accusing him of aligning with Satan.[4] Jesus was telling his accusers they must decide; either Satan was at work here, or Jesus was something special. It couldn't be both.

The Jewish people who were listening to Jesus would have instantly connected his words with the story of Rehoboam and Jeroboam—the story that marked the beginning of the downfall of Israel—an immature-teenager story that teaches us something profound about the Overall story.

Internal division happens before the collapse.

When people who are on the same team start fighting among themselves, they will experience the greatest damage. Abraham Lincoln's words proved to be eerily prophetic when, just a few years later, southern states started seceding from the Union and the Civil War broke out. More American lives were lost in that war than all other wars combined.

Internal division happens before the collapse.

The same can be said about marriage. People don't tend to explore provocative relationships at work when things are healthy at home. People usually don't initiate searches of old high-school boyfriends or girlfriends on social media when there's joy and intimacy at home.

A house divided against itself cannot stand.

The tragedy of the American Civil War connects with the concern Jesus was addressing with his adversaries. And it's the same devastation the Israelites found themselves facing. When we fight among ourselves, we lose track of who the enemy is. There's a real enemy in the story—the third character—and he wants nothing more than for us to engage in internal division. Recall the two levels on the stage from Chapter 1.1. If we are unaware of the supernatural (upper) level or forget it exists, then our only option is to identify an enemy from the natural (lower) level. When we are fighting with each other, we have little or no resistance to offer the true enemy at our borders.

When the Northern kingdom was battling the Southern kingdom, would that have been an advantage or disadvantage to the Philistines who were west of both kingdoms along the Mediterranean coast? or to the Moabites or Edomites to the east? It was obviously an advantage, so why give it to them? Asa was one of the kings of Judah (South). He removed silver and gold from the temple and gave them to a neighboring nation so it could help fight with them against the king of Israel (North).[5] This was a lose-lose situation.

Internal division creates confusion as to who the real enemy is. God is the protagonist. We are his beloved. And Satan is the enemy. Your boss is not the enemy. Your spouse is not the enemy. If you're divorced, your ex is not the enemy. If you are a teenager, your parents are not the enemy. They may have terrible taste in clothes and music, but they are not the enemy:

> *Our struggle is not against flesh and blood, but against the rulers, against the authorities, against the powers of this dark world and against the spiritual forces of evil in the heavenly realms. —Ephesians 6:12*

In this and the next three chapters, the goal is not to *understand* the exile that resulted from profound violation. The goal is to build more framework so we can understand the Overall story and increase our adoration of the protagonist. The only way to understand *this* part of the story—the second half of the Old Testament, these writings that make up such a large portion of the Bible—is to unpack the exile. It's a means to a life-changing end.

1. The Assyrian Empire was one of the earliest empires and occupied portions of modern-day Iraq as well as parts of Iran, Kuwait, Syria, and Turkey. It was famous for conquering territories and relocating entire populations from their homes.
2. Babylon was a beautiful and lavish city located about fifty miles south of modern-day Baghdad. The Babylonians were at their most powerful state when they conquered Jerusalem, but fell soon after to the Persians.
3. The classic *Hans and Franz* tagline.
4. Mark 3:25.
5. 2 Chronicles 16:1–3.

2.2 Warning

I was out for dinner with my wife and daughter when I got a call from my sixteen-year-old son who was out with his friends, driving my car. The conversation went something like this.

"Dad, something's wrong with the car."

"What happened?"

"I filled it up with gas, then less than a mile down the road, it started sputtering. So I turned in to a parking lot and shut the engine off."

"Was there anything wrong with it before you filled it up?"

"I don't think so."

"Did you do anything different at the gas station?"

"I don't think so."

"Son, what was the color of the nozzle you used to fill the car with?"

"Uh—I think it was green."

"That's diesel fuel. You put diesel fuel in a gasoline engine. But I'm confused because the nozzle is a different size and shouldn't even fit in the hole."

"Yeah. I had to jam it in there. I thought that was a little strange."

A $1,600 flush and a new catalytic converter later, all was well. My son and I have discussed this moment multiple times. His position is, "You didn't *tell* me not to put diesel in the car."

And my response remains, "I also didn't tell you not to put chocolate milk in the gas tank, but I didn't think that was necessary."

From generation to generation, the teenage brain is not fully developed.

Teens need guidance as they explore their new freedoms. We tell them, "Here's a new phone. It will make your world much bigger. But I must put limitations on the phone because you do not yet know how powerful it is. It's not your phone, it's mine. And if you choose to misuse it, I will take it away from you." Teenagers are excited to explore, but they must hear the warnings. Later we tell them, "Here are the keys to the car. It will make your world much bigger. But this incredibly powerful machine is the number-one killer of sixteen-to-eighteen-year-olds." Here is something wonderful and powerful, and here is a warning so that you will hopefully handle it well.

God said to the teenage nation of Israel, "Here is the Promised Land. Here are tremendous power, wealth, and influence. Enjoy it all, but remember the laws and the rules. Here are very clear warnings of what will happen if you violate them or if you misuse all that I have provided for you." That's not vengeful deism. That's good parenting.

The Role of the Prophets

The message of the prophets was a warning:

> *The Lord warned Israel and Judah through all his prophets and seers: "Turn from your evil ways. Observe my commands and decrees, in accordance with the entire Law that I commanded your ancestors to obey and that I delivered to you through my servants the prophets." —2 Kings 17:13*

God is not trying to "catch" us doing something wrong. He lovingly provides us with every possible opportunity to make good decisions. He provides us with warning and warning after warning, but sometimes warnings are not well-received.

I'm not a fan of the *ding…ding* noise my car makes as a reminder for me to put my seatbelt on. If I fail to oblige within ten seconds, it shifts into double-time.

Ding, ding, ding, ding.

Out of concern for my well-being, my daughter has decided she should correct me along with the car's seatbelt warning. In unison with the car, she says, "Dad…Dad."

Then double-time: "Dad, Dad, Dad, Dad."

She and her mother enjoy this very much. For me, it's annoying in stereo.

The role of the prophets was a difficult one. They had a message of truth from God for a group of people who often didn't want to hear it. This tension and resistance are why the prophets sometimes come across as odd characters:

- Isaiah walked around naked for three years as a warning against Egypt.[1]
- Ezekiel lay on his side for 390 days, then ate bread baked over cow manure.[2]
- Hosea married an unfaithful prostitute as a message to the North (Israel).[3]

These guys were peculiar, and they didn't get invited to many parties.

The prophets were burdened with the ability to see what others could not or did not want to see. They were like a hidden camera in the kitchen of your favorite restaurant. You don't want to see the chef sneezing, or wiping his nose, or picking food up off the ground, blowing on it, and returning it to the grill. You just want your meal hot and tasty.

Prophets were like the shuttle bus from the airport to your hotel on the beach. In many resort destinations in impoverished countries, this drive forces us to see the devastating poverty that is just beyond the view of the hotel. We don't want to see that. We want to see the beach and our beautiful room. For this reason, some of these shuttles have windows that are blacked out. We don't want to see what the prophet sees. We don't want to hear what the prophet has to say.

A Couple of Examples

The role of the prophet was a difficult job.

Jeremiah was one of the four major prophets. He lived in the South (Judah) and God called him to warn his people about the possibility of exile:

> *"Stand up and say to them whatever I command you.... Today I have made you a fortified city...against the kings of Judah, its officials, its priests and the people of the land. They will fight against you but will not overcome you, for I am with you and will rescue you." —Jeremiah 1:17–19*

Jeremiah started off strong. He smashed a clay jar in front of the leaders and said that would be their fate if they did not turn back to God.[4]

> *When the priest Pashhur son of Immer, the official in charge of the temple of the LORD, heard Jeremiah prophesying these things, he had Jeremiah the prophet beaten and put in the stocks at the Upper Gate of Benjamin at the LORD's temple. —Jeremiah 20:1–2*

Not exactly what Jeremiah had in mind when he signed up for the job. And it didn't get any easier for him. People didn't want to hear what the prophet had to say.

Amos was one of the twelve minor prophets. He was a shepherd from the South who had a warning for the people of the North (Israel). He gathered a large audience in a public area in the North and started shouting warnings against their neighboring nations who were violating God's laws. He started with Damascus to the north, then Gaza to the southwest, then Tyre to the northwest. With each neighboring nation, he would yell an indictment of them, and the people likely responded with a roaring cheer of satisfaction. It was like a pep rally, and he was degrading all the opposing teams.

Then he got to Judah in the south and the people went crazy. The kingdom was divided, and these were the arch-rivals of the North.

"Yeah! Destroy them Judah-sissies! Let's go burn their mascot!"

Amos then added one final nation to his list of people who were to be given a harsh warning from God. And this one was the longest warning. All the others were two verses; this one was eleven. It was a warning against the people gathered to listen to Amos—a warning against the North (Israel) itself:

> *"They trample on the heads of the poor*
> *as on the dust of the ground*
> *and deny justice to the oppressed....*
>
> *"Now then, I will crush you*
> *as a cart crushes when loaded with grain.*
> *The swift will not escape,*
> *the strong will not muster their strength,*
> *and the warrior will not save his life." —Amos 2:7, 13–14*

And the crowd went silent.

People don't want to hear what the prophet has to say.

Step Back from the Edge

What if the message of the prophet had been embraced instead of resisted? What if the people responded like appreciative adults instead of entitled teenagers?

Have you ever been pulled over by the police, investigated for a few moments, then blessed with those beautiful words, "I'm just going to give you a warning"? A warning is a terrific thing because it means there's still time to change. Over ninety percent of the prophetic writings in the Old Testament were visions of an avoidable future, not an inevitable one. Warnings provide us with an opportunity to adjust.

Imagine your life played out on a field near the edge of a steep cliff. How close to the edge do you want to play? Are you curious and want to know what lies beyond the boundary, or do you keep your distance?

For many, the edge is exciting and provocative. They don't want to tumble over the cliff, but they want the excitement of being close. Everything is fine if they are perfectly steady as they walk along the edge. But the reality of life is that we trip. We make mistakes. We have bad days. When we stumble and we are far from the edge, we have plenty of room to recover. But even a slight stumble right at the edge can lead to disaster.

In my marriage, I want to stay far away from the edge. There's not necessarily anything wrong with having lunch or dinner with another woman as part of my job or as a way of connecting with an old friend.

But I choose not to do it because most affairs start off with an innocent, intimate, enjoyable conversation. If it looks like a date, smells like a date, and feels like a date—it's not a duck.

We all have warning lights that come on as we approach the cliff. How close do you have to be before you hear:

Ding...ding.

How close do you have to be before the warning shifts into double-time?

Ding, ding, ding, ding.

I've never known anyone who regretted keeping a good distance from the edge. I've known plenty who have intensely regretted getting too close.

What Kind of Person Are You?

Remember, the first character in the Overall story relentlessly takes steps to reconcile and connect with the second character. The third character uses every conceivable tactic to get in the way.

The antagonist lures us to the edge. Satan invites us to come check it out—to look over the cliff and experience the excitement of spiritual danger and emotional risk. Then when we cross the line, he (and most of the world) says, "What kind of person are you? Shame on you! How could you have done that?"

It's entice, entice, entice...shame.

The protagonist has the opposite message. God provides us with guidelines and boundaries and wants us to stay away from the edge. *Before* we cross the line, he says: "What kind of person are you? Whom do you want to be? Whom do you trust?"

Then when we stumble, God offers love and grace.

The thirty-ninth chapter in the Book of Isaiah tells the tragic story of the Babylonian exile for the people of Jerusalem. It came after many, many warnings. And the first words in the next chapter of Isaiah are:

> *Comfort, comfort my people,*
> *says your God.*
> *Speak tenderly to Jerusalem,*
> *and proclaim to her*
> *that her hard service has been completed.* —*Isaiah 40:1–2*

The very first word after the exile is *comfort.*

Instead of entice, entice, entice…shame, God's message is warning, warning, warning…comfort.

The teenage nation of Israel did not want to stay clear of the edge. They didn't pay attention to the warnings. They drove around in their beautiful, expensive car and put black tape over the "check engine" light because it was annoying.

God did not want to send them into exile. He loved them dearly and gave them every opportunity to avoid it. What was true for them remains true for most of us: we naturally don't want to hear what the prophet has to say. But the more we engage in a relationship with God—not simply understanding the story but in an actual relationship—the more likely we are to hear and embrace the voice of the prophets.

1. Isaiah 20:2–4.
2. Ezekiel 4:4–5, 15.
3. Hosea 1:2–3.
4. Jeremiah 19.

2.3 Consequence

In 722 BC,

> *The king of Assyria invaded the entire land, marched against Samaria and laid siege to it for three years. In the ninth year of Hoshea, the king of Assyria captured Samaria and deported the Israelites to Assyria. —2 Kings 17:5–6*

In 586 BC,

> *God gave them all into the hands of Nebuchadnezzar. He carried to Babylon all the articles from the temple of God, both large and small, and the treasures of the LORD's temple and the treasures of the king and his officials. They set fire to God's temple and broke down the wall of Jerusalem; they burned all the palaces and destroyed everything of value there.*
>
> *He carried into exile to Babylon the remnant, who escaped from the sword, and they became servants to him and his successors. —2 Chronicles 36:17–20*

God did it.

He repeatedly warned his people what would happen if they violated his laws and continued to ignore him. And he followed through. The exile was far from pleasant. They didn't just pack up their belongings and move from one country to another. Their temple and their homes were burned to the ground. Men were stripped away from their families and forced to use their skills for the nations that captured them. Thousands of people died making the arduous trip across the desert to Assyria and Babylon. Over seven hundred years of growth and development for the nation of Israel in the Promised Land—shattered.

Broken.

Exiled.

It didn't happen because God was not powerful enough to stop it. God is the one who did it. He kicked his teenage nation out of the house.

How does that make you feel about God as the protagonist in the grand story? Did you ever experience significant consequences as a teenager? Were you ever kicked out? Were you ever grounded and missed a critical event? Did you ever spend time in a holding cell or juvie?

Parents Need to Follow Through

Most families can identify the *spoiled one* in the family. They might not talk about it, but they all know. It's often the youngest sibling. If you're not sure who it is in your family, it's probably you. My two older brothers think I'm the spoiled one, but that isn't true. I'm not spoiled—I'm special.

Ha.

Spoilage occurs when kids don't experience consequences for their actions, and it has been happening since the beginning of time.

> *Whoever spares the rod hates their children,*
> *but the one who loves their children is careful to discipline them. —Proverbs 13:24*

Rod-sparing is motivated by love. Parents want their kids to be happy and have everything their hearts desire. Which, of course, is the problem. A loving parent is strong enough to discipline a child just as a loving God is bold enough to follow through on consequences to his people.

Among my kids and their friends, I have a reputation for providing frequent mini-lectures. I think that word clarifies that these are rarely well-received. Years ago, I was driving while two of our kids were in the back seat. My daughter quietly reminded her brother to put his seatbelt on, which reminded me that mine was not on either.

For reference, this was before we bought the car with the lovely *ding…ding* warning.

I tried to slip my seatbelt on quietly to be unnoticed, then cleverly delivered a discreet "cough" while I snapped the buckle.

Genius, I know.

They didn't fall for it and chuckled at my efforts. To their relief, I smiled and enjoyed the moment with them. My son said, "Whew, I thought we were going to get a lecture."

I asked, "Do I give lectures?"

Silence.

They were both concerned that their next words would trigger a lecture about the importance of words of wisdom from loving adults. I have learned as a parent that my words are not as helpful as I imagine them to be. My kids know when they have done something wrong. They don't need to hear, once again, what the rules are about TV time, or video games, or sugary cereal. They don't need more lectures. They need clear expectations and fair consequences. They need parents to be clear about the plan, then follow through on that plan.

Teenagers Need Consequences

Teenagers are awesome. They look at something dangerous and see a challenge. They look at something mundane and turn it into something extraordinary.

Growing up in Canada, we played a game called broomball. You put twenty to thirty teenagers on an ice-hockey rink, wearing whatever shoes or boots they put on that morning. You pull out a bin of brooms, each with a wooden shaft and a tightly wrapped head of short bristles. Divide the group into two even teams, with a hockey goal on each end of the rink. Then toss a ball with the same density of a hockey puck in the middle and see which team can score more goals. Sticks swinging. Feet slipping. No helmets. No shin pads. No sense.

Broomball is a game that must have been created by teenagers because only they would be courageous enough to play it. Adults understand consequences and that broomball is a concussion and/or lawsuit waiting to happen. Teenagers really are terrific, but they are in a stage of life where they need to learn about consequences by experiencing them.

Consequences are natural. "Con" means "with," and "sequence" means "to follow." Consequences are a natural next step. They are not an indicator of a disaster. They are an essential part of growth and development.

After We Fall

There are three things that happen after we fall—after we have blown through warning after warning, lecture after lecture, and find ourselves in exile.

1. ***Comfort.*** We learned in Chapter 2.2 that God's first response is comfort. After thirty-nine chapters of warnings in the Book of Isaiah, God's first words after the exile were, "Comfort, comfort my people." God will never say, "I told you so," or, "You got what you deserved." Loving parents hug their children after discipline to make sure they know they're cherished, first and foremost.

2. ***Punishment.*** Nahum was a minor prophet who was not addressing the North or the South. God called him to challenge the people in a city in Assyria named Nineveh:

> *The Lord is slow to anger but great in power;*
> *the Lord will not leave the guilty unpunished. —Nahum 1:3*

God is just. When rules are violated or lines are crossed, he can't simply say, "Ah, don't worry about it." This is a good thing. Justice is a very good thing because it means the innocent will be protected.

3. ***Consequences.*** Consequences are different from punishment. Consequences naturally follow the mistakes we make, whereas punishment is an action taken by a higher power. When (not if) someone slips in broomball and smashes his or her head on the ice, that's not punishment. It's a natural consequence of the decision to play the life-threatening game.

We looked at the prophet Jeremiah in Chapter 2.2. He had a very difficult journey, but he provided one of the most beloved verses in all of the Scriptures:

> *"For I know the plans I have for you," declares the LORD, "plans to prosper you and not to harm you, plans to give you hope and a future." —Jeremiah 29:11*

These are inspiring words, but they are typically used out of context. Prior to this verse, a prophet-wannabe named Hananiah declared that God said the people would return from exile after two years. But the true prophet, Jeremiah, said on behalf of God,

> *"When seventy years are completed for Babylon, I will come to you and fulfill my good promise to bring you back to this place." —Jeremiah 29:10*

He said this immediately before the cherished words in verse 11. Yes, God had a terrific plan of restoration, but it wasn't going to happen in two years. It was going to be seventy. That was multiple generations. That was far beyond the need to endure Babylon for a short while. That was settling in. This was not punishment from God. It was the natural consequence of being wiped out by a pagan nation. Yes, comfort is instant, but relief is not. There are consequences.

Looking Ahead

Allow me to jump ahead briefly for a moment. The exile is a critical part of the story for Bible-readers to be familiar with, but it is not the full story. What we discover through the story of Jesus is an adjustment to the three things that happen after we fall.

1. ***Comfort.*** Comfort still happens immediately. Jesus is described as "full of grace and truth."[1] The truth part is the warning: There's a cliff ahead of you—stay away from it and be careful. The grace part is the comfort: If you sail over the cliff, I will be there to care for you.[2]

2. ***Punishment.*** This is the part that is radically different. It remains true that "somebody must pay." God is still just and can't say, "Ah, don't worry about it." What we discover in the story of Jesus is that somebody already *has* paid. That's why Jesus' death on the cross was so brutal. Jesus paid the punishment for every person who has ever stumbled or jumped off any cliff.

3. *Consequences.* Jesus took care of the punishment but not the consequences. For this reason,

- A college student who cheats can be allowed to finish her degree, but still lose her scholarship.
- A person addicted to sex can have ten successful years of recovery, but still have no computer or phone privacy.
- A woman who committed adultery can be smothered in grace, but still lose her marriage.
- Someone who molests a child can be embraced by a loving support group, but still be on the national registry for twenty-five years.
- An alcoholic can experience the power of freedom from his addiction, but still lose his job.

God's comfort is immediate. Jesus' grace is unstoppable. But there will often be consequences to our poor choices.

1. John 1:14.
2. See *The Grace and Truth Paradox* by Randy Alcorn (Colorado Springs: Multnomah Press, 1992), 87–88.

2.4 Restoration

I'm a car guy. I love going to shows and listening to owners tell their "restories" of taking a jalopy and turning it into a beautiful piece of automotive art. I'm not impressed with a new car that looks just like the one parked next to it, but I love a restored classic.

Tami and I don't share the same perspective on this topic. She drives a late-model Honda, while I drive a 1967 Volkswagen Bus. She likes to hop in her car and expect it to start every time rather than hope it will start. She likes to arrive at her destination and not smell like oil and gas. She thinks it's foolish for a man who is over six feet tall to fold into a small, uncomfortable seat that doesn't adjust, then drive a vehicle with poor brakes, no airbags, and no air conditioning in the heat of the Arizona desert.

You can see how unreasonable she can be.

Your life is a classic. You've been around for several years, and you've experienced multiple dings, dents, accidents, and breakdowns. You need restoration by a master craftsman so that you can return to the person you were designed to be.

"I Will Restore Them"

We're nearing the end of the Old Testament story. Because of their violation, the people of God had been in exile in a foreign land for seventy years—multiple generations. All of us are familiar with the consequences of poor choices. All of us have been in exile at some point, and you may be in exile right now:

- Waiting for your kids to decide what kind of relationship they want to have with you.
- Waiting for the next employer to give you another chance.

- Waiting for something to change so you can break through your negative patterns.

Comfort is wonderful and it's what we need the instant we stumble over the edge. But as we navigate the reality of consequences, what we desire is the hope of restoration. God provided this encouragement to his struggling people:

> *"The days are coming," declares the* Lord, *"when it will no longer be said, 'As surely as the* Lord *lives, who brought the Israelites up out of Egypt,' but it will be said, 'As surely as the* Lord *lives, who brought the Israelites up out of the land of the north and out of all the countries where he had banished them.' For I will restore them to the land I gave their ancestors." —Jeremiah 16:14–15*

God made a promise that every exiled soul wants to hear: "I will restore them."

As children, God's people celebrated the miracle of Moses and the parting of the Red Sea. As teenagers, they would celebrate the return from exile. God's jalopy of a nation was about to be restored. A group of people—thousands of Israelites—would return to Jerusalem to begin the restoration process, but they were not fully successful.

The Old Testament story promises full restoration, but it doesn't provide it.

Three Phases

The return from exile happened in three phases that are recorded in two books: Ezra and Nehemiah. Though this is the end of the Old Testament story, these books are found in the middle because the general order of the Old Testament is:

- One Nation story (Genesis through 1 Kings)
- Violation story (1 Kings through Esther)
- One Nation writings (Job through Song of Songs)
- Violation writings (Isaiah through Malachi—i.e., the prophets)

Phase I: *The Temple.* The first phase was the rebuilding of the temple by Zerubbabel. I highly encourage you to say that name out loud because it's a gem. My hope is that expecting parents of a baby boy will be inspired.

Zer-OO-buh-BEL.

They cleared away the rubble from Solomon's temple and built the new temple on the exact same spot. They began with the house of God. In the center of the city, they started with a visible reminder that said, "We can't do this without God." It was like the first three steps in a modern twelve-step recovery program, and it was a great place to start.

But—the new temple was dwarfed by memories of the old temple:

> *Many of the older priests and Levites and family heads, who had seen the former temple, wept aloud when they saw the foundation of this temple being laid. —Ezra 3:12*

The Old Testament promises full restoration, but it doesn't provide it.

Phase II: *The Law.* The second phase was led by Ezra, who was a priest and an expert in the Law. He wanted to make sure people remembered and understood the boundaries and guidelines from Moses that were provided in Part I (One Nation). He reminded them that the exile happened because God's people violated the Law. The people gathered as Ezra prayed to God,

> *"We have forsaken the commands you gave through your servants the prophets." —Ezra 9:10–11*

Sadly, generation after generation has proven that we can't uphold these laws. We can all do well with some of them for a period, but it's not sustainable.

The Old Testament promises full restoration, but it doesn't provide it.

Phase III: *The Walls.* Thirdly, we have the terrific leadership of Nehemiah. He left the comfort and prosperity of a high position in Persia[1] because he felt called to return to Jerusalem to rebuild the walls around the city. But he was met with significant opposition. The leaders in and around Jerusalem wanted to retain their political and economic strength. Nehemiah offered an insightful request to God:

> *"Now strengthen my hands." —Nehemiah 6:9*

This brief phrase captures the balance between God's role and our role in the restoration process. We are not to just sit back with a cold drink and watch God do the work for us. Neither are we to take control and let God know if we need him. The rebuilding of the walls requires my hands, empowered by God's strength.

The task was daunting. The wall was over two miles long and would unlikely be completed by the assembled crew. Nehemiah asked each family along the wall to rebuild their small section.[2] The whole wall might seem impossible, but this section in front of me seems doable—especially when I ask God to "strengthen my hands."

This balance is reinforced later in the story. The families experienced relentless opposition, but Nehemiah encouraged the builders to do the work with one hand and carry a weapon in the other.[3] The enemy doesn't pause while we make efforts to strengthen our walls. He will eagerly take the opportunity to discourage, mock, or entice long before we are ready to resist.

Through exceptional leadership and a prayer for God to strengthen their hands, the walls were built.

But—we can't build walls high enough to protect us from all enemies. As the saying goes, "Wherever you go, there you are."[4] You'll always have your weaknesses, your insecurities, and your temptations. The people of God were reasonably safe in Jerusalem for the time being, but they were still under Persian rule. Then the Greeks took over, led by Alexander the Great, only to be overpowered years later by Pompey, who put Israel under Roman control.

The Old Testament promises full restoration, but it doesn't provide it.

Unfinished

After I shared the story of Nehemiah at the church I was pastoring in Phoenix, Arizona, I came across a very upset woman named Shelley who had found out that week that her husband had been cheating on her for years. She thought she was living in "Jerusalem," but was suddenly catapulted into exile. The wound was too fresh to imagine or consider restoration. She was upset with the idea of asking God to "strengthen her hands" as she fought this battle. She wasn't interested in grace, forgiveness, or reconciliation. She wanted fire to rain down from heaven and smite her adulterous husband.

My words, not hers.

She was sweetly broken and simply said, "I disagree with you, pastor."

I held her hands and said, "It's always okay to disagree with me. God is the one you want to line up with. You're going to be fine, Shelley. Your church will not abandon you and we will not pick sides. But can you ask God to strengthen your hands and remain open to the possibility of miraculous restoration?"

In the reality of our brokenness and our seasons of exile, it's not enough to enter a temple, remember the laws, and build walls. The restoration outlined in the Old Testament is unfinished. The story is incomplete. The promise is unfulfilled.

Even from a Jewish perspective—which views the story thus far as the complete Hebrew Bible—the story is unfinished. Jewish people celebrate Passover and leave an empty chair for the possible return of Elijah, who was one of the prophets during the divided kingdom. And they continue to wait for the Messiah who is described in detail by the prophet Isaiah. What Christians refer to as the "Old Testament" is an unfinished story.

Many Christians are inclined to teach through Old Testament stories as if they are complete. But they're not. We can learn from King David, but we can't get the full story of God from his life. We can learn from Ezra and Nehemiah and Isaiah and Ezekiel—but their stories are incomplete.

As Jeremiah was warning the people of Jerusalem before the exile, he was given a glimpse of what full restoration would look like:

> *"The days are coming," declares the* L*ORD,*
> *"when I will raise up for David a righteous Branch,*
> *a King who will reign wisely*
> *and do what is just and right in the land.*
> *In his days Judah will be saved*
> *and Israel will live in safety.*
> *This is the name by which he will be called:*
> *The* L*ORD Our Righteous Savior." —Jeremiah 23:5–6*

The Old Testament story is unfinished. Something is missing.

After a few years, Shelley and her husband took tiny restoration steps consistent with the phases found in the Books of Ezra and Nehemiah. They stayed connected at church (temple); they remained obedient to the ways of God (law); and they slowly rebuilt trust, one stone at a time (walls). But something was missing.

What we will discover in the upcoming chapters is that something needed to be added to Part I (One Nation) and Part II (Violation). The story thus far has introduced the characters and set the stage for the crux of the story—the "Righteous Savior."

1. The Babylonians conquered Jerusalem, the central city of Judah, in 586 BC. But they only lasted another fifty years before they were taken over by the Persians.
2. Nehemiah 3.
3. Nehemiah 4:17.
4. The earliest version of this saying is found in the Thomas à Kempis book *The Imitation of Christ* from the early 1400s, where he wrote, "You cannot escape it, run where you will; for wherever you go, you take yourself with you, and you will always find yourself."

PART III: **EMMANUEL**

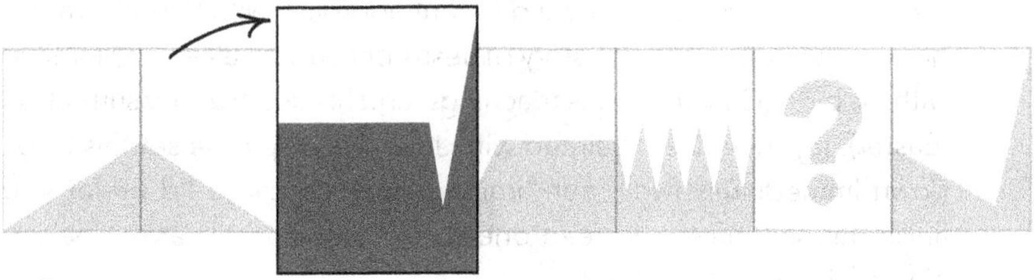

Emmanuel: Jesus' life, death, and resurrection

Intro

Can you recall a wonderful moment in life when you sat back with your hands behind your head and sighed, "Ahh, this is what it's all about"?

- Sitting on the beach in Hawaii
- Enjoying a long, challenging hike in Colorado
- Gliding through powder while skiing in the Canadian Rockies
- Enjoying a grate book free of annoying typos

Ahh, this is the life!

I hope you've been blessed with moments such as these. But if those moments have nothing to do with Jesus, then we are simply chasing shiny objects. The overall point of human existence is knowing Jesus and doing what he says. We can do that on the beach, on a hike, or on the slopes—but *that* is the life.

Jesus is literally the crux of the story. *Crux* is a Latin word that originally referred to an instrument of torture—a cross or a stake. It's the root of the word *crucifixion*. Jesus is the crux of the story. He's the main point, the main idea, the main argument. God came from the upper stage and became one of us on the lower stage. Everything we find in the Old Testament leads up to this, and everything that has happened since flows from it.

Emmanuel is one of the titles given to Jesus and it literally means, "God with us."[1] The first character in the Overall story is not leading from afar. He became flesh because he genuinely wants a relationship *with us*.

Because of this, I'm taking a different approach with Part III. I'm not going to walk through the *story* of Jesus because you're likely familiar with his birth (Christmas), his teachings, and his death and resurrection (Easter). If you're unacquainted with Jesus' story, please set this book down immediately (well, not "immediately," because I'd prefer you finish this sentence) and read one of the four Gospels at the beginning of the New Testament:

- Read Matthew if you want to focus on what Jesus taught.
- Read Mark if you're in a hurry.
- Read Luke if you want the most complete and detailed version.
- Read John if you're a right-brained, Psalms person.

I'm focusing on "God with us" because it's much more important to *know* Jesus than it is to know *about* him. Jesus is not a story; he's a person. What if the elusive concept of spiritual growth is essentially just spending time with Jesus—hanging out with him and getting to know him?

Human relationships happen naturally. I didn't have to read a book about Tami before I began my relationship with her. I simply wanted to be with her. She was willing to tolerate me, and we naturally spent time together.

Experts help us understand human relationships by saying that we go through "stages" such as passion, commitment, struggles, and recovery. Different experts identify different stages because the whole idea is not systematic. What if our relationship with Jesus goes through similar stages? If an encounter with Jesus is real, then perhaps we will experience relational stages with him.

1. Matthew 1:23. There are two spellings of this name given to Jesus. *Immanuel* is a transliteration of the original Hebrew word whereas *Emmanuel* is from the Greek. It's kind of like *Allan* versus *Allen*. Or *Chloe* versus *Klowee*.

3.1 Decision Stage

When my kids were little, I shared goofy stories about me and my best friend, Darryl. Darryl and I met in middle school and navigated life together until each of us got married. I once fed him Ex-Lax and told him it was chocolate candy because I thought it would be funny. We laugh about it now, but he didn't think it was super funny that night. He once bet that I could not eat ten Dairy Queen Royal Treat desserts in one sitting. I foolishly tried but stopped at seven-and-a-half before vomiting on the way home while he laughed hysterically. You know, regular guy stuff.

Darryl and I listened to a lot of Paul Simon together, and I still enjoy the line from the song "Late in the Evening" where Simon mentions feeling good as he walks down the street with "my boys" and refers to them as "my troops."

It's a powerful and coveted thing to have deep relationships. To have *troops*.

Jesus had twelve buddies. He's known for choosing twelve ordinary, imperfect guys to be part of his team. This is incredible. Can you think of any major leader in world history who did anything such as that? Can you name Muhammad's best friends? or Napoleon's sidekicks? or members of Gandhi's inner circle?

Jesus was a rabbi who selected twelve disciples to travel with him, to learn from him, to be *with* him.

Imagine what it would have been like to have Jesus walk up to you and say, "Follow me. Drop what you're doing, set aside your plans, and follow me." What if you were one of the fortunate twelve? Imagine eating with Jesus and knowing what he liked and didn't like. Imagine laughing with Jesus or saying something that made him laugh. Imagine being so familiar with his teachings that you could finish his sentences and his stories. Some stories you loved—others you struggled with, if you were honest.

Have you ever considered yourself one of the Twelve? Do you think it's possible to be that close to Jesus?

Levi was a Jewish man making significant shekels as a tax collector for the Roman government. Jesus looked at him and saw what others did not, which is what Jesus beautifully does with all of us:

> *"Follow me," Jesus told him, and Levi got up and followed him. —Mark 2:14*

Levi made the decision to follow Jesus, a decision that would one day cost him his life, but I don't imagine he regretted it—not even for a moment.

> *While Jesus was having dinner at Levi's house, many tax collectors and sinners were eating with him and his disciples. —Mark 2:15*

There are two kinds of people listed here: "sinners," which might include rapists, murderers, and thieves; and "tax collectors," which was a category all on its own. So, yes, Levi was certainly despised by his fellow Jews. Nonetheless, Jesus sat at his table and had a meal with him and his newly selected disciples.

> *When the teachers of the law who were Pharisees saw him eating with the sinners and tax collectors, they asked his disciples: "Why does he eat with tax collectors and sinners?" —Mark 2:16*

The Pharisees were committed to the Old Testament story and not interested in Jesus' new way. I'll return to this in a moment.

Levi was one of the Twelve. His name was changed to Matthew and, years after his time with Jesus, he wrote down his experience, which became the first book in the New Testament. Matthew wanted people to know this rabbi he had come to love. He wanted people to understand that Jesus was fully human. Jesus was not just the central character in a major world religion—he was and is a person.

Limited Information

Like the rest of the Twelve, Levi had to make a decision to follow Jesus based on limited information. He knew the stories from Parts I and II. He knew the words of the prophets and the promises of a messiah. He was painfully aware of the four hundred years of silence since Malachi, who was the last prophet and author of the last book in the Old Testament. Levi had his own tradition and engaged in conversations with his family about how the next part of the grand story would play out.

It's the same thing for us. We know so much more now, of course, but we are still dealing with limited information. We know people who call themselves "Christian" but don't seem to represent Christ well. We encounter Christians who are judgmental and more likely to point a finger than lend a hand, who are hypocritical by flipping people off from their Jesus-fish cars, who reinforce the notion that "loving Jesus" means "hating gays." At the same time, we've known some remarkable, generous, compassionate people who follow Jesus. And we've met some walking miracles who swear on their lives that they are only free or alive because of the grace and power of Jesus.

Is that enough information for us to make this life-changing decision? Is it reasonable to make a decision about Jesus solely based on those who say they follow him?

The Problem

One of the bumper stickers on the Jesus-fish car mentioned above might say *Jesus Is the Answer*. But do we even know what the question is? Perhaps you wonder about the benefit of reducing your perceived "fun" in life by submitting to the ways of Jesus.

If I may be so bold—I know what your problem is.

What brings more joy than someone starting a conversation with, "Do you know what your problem is?" Especially a stranger who is hiding behind the written word.

It's actually a terrific thing to clearly identify the problem. You can't fix something if you don't know what's wrong. I remember sitting in Mr.

Zurawell's eighth-grade science class. I was daydreaming when I heard him say, "Fuller...Fuller...what is the answer?"

My buddy Darryl saw that I was in trouble and mercifully whispered "Car...car," so I boldly used the response he provided. At that moment, the entire class burst into laughter while Darryl pounded on his desk in delight. I'll never know what Mr. Zurawell asked, but I do know that "car" was not an acceptable answer.

"Jesus" can't be the answer if we don't know what the question is.

I know what your problem is because it's the same as mine.

Control.

We all want control, but we can't have it. Children have very little control in the grocery store, so they do the only thing that's guaranteed to get mom's attention: flailing on the floor and screaming bloody murder. Teenagers face new levels of consequences because they have newfound control and don't know how to handle it. The issue with lying is always control—we want to control the narrative and manage who thinks or knows what. We want to exercise control over people who are not doing what we wish. We want control over ourselves. We want to stop actions that are self-destructive, and we want to continue ones that are healthy.

But we can't. We want to, but we can't. In the next section of this book (Part IV), we'll learn about Paul, who was a refreshingly honest writer in the Bible. He said,

> *I do not understand what I do. For what I want to do I do not do, but what I hate I do. —Romans 7:15*

We can either admit that we have a problem, or we can continue to pretend that we don't. After Jesus invited Levi to join him and shared a meal at his house, Jesus said the following to the judgmental Pharisees:

> *"It is not the healthy who need a doctor, but the sick. I have not come to call the righteous, but sinners." —Mark 2:17*

Jesus never intended to be the answer for people who weren't asking the question. He can't heal those who deny their sickness. He came to offer a solution for those who recognize there's a problem.

The Condition of Your Heart

So—do you see yourself as spiritually sick and in need of a doctor, or healthy and in need of nothing? It's not an easy question because we all have good days where we feel healthy, and it's difficult to admit we can't fight off the sickness on our own.

How about you? Do you have your *control* under control?

Jesus told a parable to help us evaluate our willingness to accept his help. A parable is a made-up story that is short, easy to connect with, and helps to make a point. Jesus was the master of parables. This one is known as the Parable of the Sower. It's about a farmer who scattered seed on four different types of soil:

> *"The farmer sows the word."* —*Mark 4:14*

The seed the farmer tosses is the story. It's the history of the Jewish people, as well as the new revelation in front of them through Jesus' words and actions. Jesus himself is even referred to as "the Word."[1] The ground represents our hearts—are we willing to accept the seed/word/truth or not?

For some, the ground is a *path*. It's packed down and doesn't allow the seed to penetrate the surface. This is a guarded heart. The enemy instills doubt and blows the seed away before it has time to penetrate the surface. This could have been Jesus' Jewish listeners. They were worn out after four hundred years of pain, struggles, and waning hope. And it is sadly the condition of many hearts today. A lot of people naturally connect the person of Jesus to "obnoxious Christians" and have no interest in who he is and what he has to offer.

For others, the ground is *rocky*. And I don't mean *Balboa*. This is a shallow heart that is looking for a quick fix. The seed springs up quickly, but it doesn't survive because there is no depth. This person will respond to a touching story about the power and mercy of Jesus, especially if it involves a good soundtrack, but interest will quickly fade away.

The ground also may be *thorny*. This is a distracted heart. The soil is ready for growth, but the seed has tremendous competition that is extremely powerful. A relationship with Jesus will not thrive if it is squeezed into the corner of a jam-packed life. When you're dating and you meet the person of your dreams, you make room for that person. Those who choose to follow Jesus must make room for him. He won't force his way in—he will let you decide what you want the relationship to look like.

The ground that is healthy and ready is *good soil.* This is where you will see growth. It takes time, but this is where you get to enjoy the fruit.

Everyone's crop is going to look a little bit different. We're not supposed to compare ourselves with one another. That would be like comparing strawberries to soybeans. It's simple, really. If you struggle identifying fruit in your life, then your heart is one of the first three types. And if that is the case, perhaps you *should* listen to Rocky Balboa, who said, "If I can change and you can change, everybody can change."[2]

Your *brain* must decide if the word/seed makes sense. Your *heart* must then be ready to embrace it.

Driving Question

John the Baptist was a strange desert-dweller who proclaimed boldly that his relative Jesus was the Messiah the Jewish people had been waiting for. He was put in prison for stirring up unrest and challenging the king's morality. While he was in prison, he had some questions. He had some obvious problems that needed some solutions. So he asked his friends to ask Jesus,

> *"Are you the one who is to come, or should we expect someone else?" —Luke 7:19*

This was John the Baptist's driving question. He knew the Hebrew story and that a messiah would come. He just wanted to find out if Jesus was the one.

When I was making the decision to follow Jesus, I had a different driving question. As I mentioned earlier, I grew up across the street from a little church in western Canada. When I was in college, a pastor asked me, "If you grew up across the street from a Muslim mosque, would you be Muslim?"

I was disturbed to discover that I had no reasonable answer. I believed wholeheartedly there was an intelligent designer of life, but how could I verify which faith system was true and which ones were less true? My driving question became, "What is the one, true, overall story of God and human existence?" I didn't want to accept Jesus because he was the only God I was introduced to, I wanted to know the grand story of life.

What is your driving question? What hole in life do you believe Jesus might fill? What do you believe is the problem, and what might it look like for Jesus to be the solution? Jesus' relationship with each person is different because our driving questions are different. As a result, he describes his role as the *solution* in a variety of different ways:

> *"Come to me, all you who are weary and burdened, and I will give you rest." —Matthew 11:28*

> *"The Son of Man did not come to be served, but to serve, and to give his life as a ransom for many." —Mark 10:45*

> *"He has sent me to proclaim freedom for the prisoners and recovery of sight for the blind." —Luke 4:18*

> *"The Son of Man came to seek and to save the lost." —Luke 19:10*

> *"I have come that they may have life, and have it to the full." —John 10:10*

> *"I have come into the world as a light, so that no one who believes in me should stay in darkness." —John 12:46*

> *"I am the way and the truth and the life." —John 14:6*

> *"The reason I was born and came into the world is to testify to the truth." —John 18:37*

> *The reason the Son of God appeared was to destroy the devil's work. —1 John 3:8*

What is your driving question? If Jesus walked up to you, looked you in the eye, and said, "Follow me," what would he have to say to convince you to drop everything?

Decision Time

The first stage in our developing relationship with Jesus is the decision stage. Will you choose to follow Jesus? You get to decide if you are one of the Twelve, sitting on the hillside, or not interested.

One of the Twelve means you get to be with Jesus. You get to sit with him, listen to him, and talk to him. You get to check in with him every day and keep him informed of the great stuff and the terrible stuff in your life. It means having an actual, personal relationship with Jesus.

Sitting on the hillside means you're one of many who are interested in Jesus but don't know him personally. Jesus would teach crowds of thousands who gathered to hear what he had to say. They heard the words of Jesus and they were influenced by those words, but they didn't know Jesus. When the event was done, when the "church service" was completed, they simply went home and continued as they were.

Not interested is likely irrelevant because you're reading this book and you've made it this far. Nonetheless, *not interested* means you don't even stop on the hillside to listen to Jesus because you don't trust or believe anything he has to say.

So—are you *one of the Twelve, sitting on the hillside*, or *not interested*?

It's your decision.

1. John 1:1.
2. End of Rocky IV.

3.2 Discovery Stage

Three years.

It's less than the time it takes to get a bachelor's degree. It's less time than the gap between *Star Wars* and *The Empire Strikes Back.*[1]

Everything we know about what Jesus said and what he did came from a three-year window of time. Every teaching, every quote, every miracle, every story.

Yes, we have details of his birth, a brief story from when he was twelve years old, and a few verses in the first chapter of Acts. But almost everything happened in three years. When you read about these three incredible years, what do you discover about who Jesus is? Reading the Gospels doesn't have to be academic. It is enjoyable to discover more about the people we like.

Tami and I met in Kenya, Africa. I was one of the drivers who picked her and her team up from the little airport in Kisumu and brought them back to the village where we were staying. She thought I was a local because I was seemingly comfortable with the twenty words I knew in Swahili. She ended up in the back seat of my Jeep and in a loud, over-enunciated voice, the first words she ever said to me were, "Have. You. Ever. Been. To. America?"

She was with me in that village for two weeks and we stayed up foolishly late each evening talking and playing games with whoever wanted to hang out with us. The night before she and her team departed, she and I walked down a variety of dirt roads until the sun came up. We found out later how ridiculously unsafe that was, both in terms of wild animals and violent locals. But Tami and I were unconcerned because of how much we enjoyed asking each other questions and listening to each other's answers. It's a wonderful part of the courtship process.

Could you imagine spending a day with Jesus? Not a one-hour interview so you could ask your burning question, but an extended period of time during which you could enjoy what he says, what he laughs at, and how he responds to the servers at the restaurant.

Matthew, Mark, Luke, John

One of the ways we get to spend time with Jesus is by absorbing the three-year story of his time as a rabbi of twelve young men. There are four authorized versions of Jesus' story, and each was written by someone who had a unique relationship with him. These four versions are found at the beginning of the New Testament and are referred to as the four *Gospels*, which means "good news." We can see some of that uniqueness in the first few verses of each Gospel.

Matthew, the tax collector previously known as Levi, wrote,

> *This is the genealogy of Jesus the Messiah the son of David, the son of Abraham. —Matthew 1:1*

Matthew was targeting a Jewish audience. He wanted to make sure people understand that Jesus is not a new story. Jesus didn't come *instead* of the promised messiah; he *is* the Messiah. He didn't come to abolish the sacred laws; he came to fulfill them. Multiple times, Matthew's Gospel uses a phrase such as, "All this took place to fulfill what the Lord had said through the prophet…."

Matthew starts by connecting with the richness of the Old Testament story.

Mark was the earliest of the Gospel writers and his work was a major source for both Matthew and Luke, which explains why significant sections are repeated word-for-word. Plagiarism wasn't an issue. They simply wanted to make sure the story got out.

Mark was the yadda-yadda Gospel writer. If you're in a rush or just want the basics, start with Mark because his version moves quickly. By the end of the first chapter, Jesus is already baptized, tempted in the desert, calling his first disciples, driving out evil spirits, healing people, and in need of a rest. Mark's story explodes out of a cannon.

Mark decided to approach the story with a sense of urgency.

Luke has the distinction of being the only clearly identifiable Gentile (non-Jewish) writer in the New Testament. His Gospel begins:

> *Many have undertaken to draw up an account of the things that have been fulfilled among us.... With this in mind, since I myself have carefully investigated everything from the beginning, I too decided to write an orderly account...so that you may know the certainty of the things you have been taught. —Luke 1:1, 3–4*

Luke was a physician and he valued accuracy. He was writing to fellow Gentiles who didn't know the Jewish story. If Gentiles were invited to say "yes" or "no" to a relationship with Jesus, it was critical for them to have accurate information. He wanted his readers to base their decision on what Jesus said and did, rather than on rumors about Jesus.

John's version could be described as the "Maverick Gospel"—likely because his writing is completely independent of the first three, but possibly because he didn't want to lose "that loving feeling." It begins:

> *In the beginning was the Word, and the Word was with God, and the Word was God. He was with God in the beginning. Through him all things were made; without him nothing was made that has been made. —John 1:1–3*

John was a poet and wrote about his time with Jesus in beautifully artistic ways. His Gospel uniquely describes Jesus as the bread of life, the light of the world, the gate, the good shepherd, the life, and the vine. He also wanted people to understand the simplicity of the good news. God loves us so much that he sent Jesus, and we are to respond by loving one another.

I would very much like to meet John because he seems like a quirky character. In his version of Jesus' resurrection, the most significant moment in the history of the world, a woman found the empty tomb and:

> *... she came running to Simon Peter and the other disciple, the one Jesus loved. —John 20:2*

John chose to take this moment to describe *himself* as the one Jesus loved. He was one of the Twelve and wanted all of humanity to know where he stood in the pecking order. He continued in the next couple of verses:

> *So Peter and the other disciple started for the tomb. Both were running, but the other disciple outran Peter and reached the tomb first. —John 20:3–4*

John also wanted all of humanity to know that he was faster than Peter. I love this guy. If you have never read a book from the Bible, John is a great place to start. His writing is real and it's thoughtful, and he spent countless hours hanging out with Jesus.

If you choose to spend time with Jesus—either by reading about him or talking directly to him—then I am confident that you will discover the following.

He Is Humble

Jesus introduced humility to the world. It didn't exist in the Old Testament story as a valued character trait. People were certainly *humbled*, but they didn't *choose* humility. The notion of lifting others up above yourself is unnatural. With few exceptions, the world has come to realize the beauty of humility because of the three-year story of Jesus. He had the power to stop the religious leaders from condemning him and the Roman soldiers from torturing him. But he didn't. He humbled himself on a cross.[2]

In chapters five through seven of Matthew's version of Jesus' story, the author provided us with the greatest and most influential speech human ears have ever heard. It's known as the Sermon on the Mount, and it's essentially a treatise on humility. Jesus taught his followers that they can either *be humbled* by their circumstances, or they can release their pride and *humble themselves.*

Jesus encouraged those who are *humbled*: the poor, those who mourn, the meek, those who are persecuted. We have all experienced a moment or a season of forced humility. Pastors have periodic Sundays we refer to as I'll-never-preach-again Sundays. It happens when a sermon is weak, and everyone knows it. There's an odd, unspoken feeling in the lobby where people seem to be thinking, "Let's pretend that didn't happen."

A splash of humility is a good wake-up call; an ocean of humility can be devastating. So we naturally avoid it.

As we get older, it becomes very difficult to learn how to play an instrument or speak a different language because the early stages are awfully humbling. We don't like that feeling of being unable to think, work, or pay our way out of a situation. But Jesus loves it when we're in that awkward place. Jesus refers to those who are forced to be humbled as "blessed," because he meets with us intimately during those awkward moments.

And to those who are prideful, Jesus challenges them to *humble themselves*. Throughout the Sermon on the Mount, he repeatedly said, "You have heard that it was said to the people long ago.... But *I* tell you...."

Jesus raises the bar. He ups the ante. He understands the destructive power of pride and he wants us to humble ourselves and break free from it. If life has not forced us to be humble, are we willing to choose humility for ourselves? A rather wealthy and intelligent woman once parked her Mercedes at our church on a Sunday morning and wanted to see what this "Jesus" thing was all about. After three Sundays, she concluded that "church" was filled with a bunch of losers who needed a crutch. Months later, she shared with me that as she was driving home, she sensed God saying, "Yes, but so are you. You're just a *sophisticated* loser."

Jesus modeled humility. He loved the unlovable, ate with tax collectors and sinners, and washed the feet of his disciples. We can either enjoy his favor when we are humbled by circumstances, or we can do the much more difficult task of humbling ourselves:

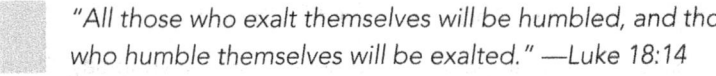

> *"All those who exalt themselves will be humbled, and those who humble themselves will be exalted."* —*Luke 18:14*

He Is Generous

If you spend any time with Jesus, you'll also discover that he is extravagantly generous. Creation itself is generous. We get to enjoy ferocious five-hundred-pound cats that dominate in the wild as well as adorable kittens that dominate online videos. There are 15,000 types of butterflies and 400,000 species of beetles.

Jesus' mom knew her son had to eventually let people know who he was. At a wedding, they ran out of wine. She walked up to a servant, nodded to Jesus, and said,

"Do whatever he tells you." —John 2:5

That's a good general rule when it comes to Jesus.

What we discover about Jesus is that he is generous, but he's not necessarily fair. It would have been fair to let the party fade because the hosts didn't have enough wine. It would have been beyond fair to turn water into cheap wine and let the festivities continue. It was way beyond fair to bless the party with choice wine. It was generous to the bride and groom, but unfair to the hypothetical sister of the bride who ran out of wine at her wedding six months earlier. Jesus is generous, not fair. He tells a similar story where people who worked a full day received the same wages as those who only worked the last hour. And another where a wayward son returned home to an extravagant celebration while the faithful son who never left was given no special treatment.

Fair is contractual and robotic. Generosity, by definition, is not fair. But it's incredibly attractive.

I recently had lunch with a table full of people including Steve Sjogren, who is the author of *Conspiracy of Kindness* and, more importantly, a rabid practitioner of generosity. Steve intended to pay for the whole tab, but someone else beat him to it. We were all thankful, but Steve was a little miffed because he enjoyed the waiter and wanted to bless him with a beyond-fair tip. So he ordered a soda to-go and added an extravagant tip onto that second bill. It was ridiculous. It was financially irresponsible. And it was beautiful to watch.

Generosity is always appealing. I've never heard anyone say, "She seems like a nice person, but she's just a little too—*generous*." When I think of the spiritual heroes in my life, they are all generous, because they know and follow a Rabbi who models it with perfection.

He Is Gracious

If Jesus had a car, he would not drive the way I drive.

Whatever gains I seem to make in terms of character development tend to vanish when I get behind the wheel. For some reason, I become patrol officer, prosecuting attorney, judge, and jury for those who drive in a way that displeases me. If I'm on a long, one-lane ramp with concrete barriers on both sides and someone rides my rear bumper as a message for me to speed up, I don't respond like someone who loves people. I drive very cautiously and remove my foot from the gas pedal. Yes, I'm that guy. And yes, I would be aggravated if I was the one driving the car behind me. It's simply a response I feel unable to control. Moments like this cause my wife to sink down in her seat, close her eyes, and pray to be transported into another vehicle.

I have moments when I don't personify graciousness. Jesus, wonderfully, does not have such moments. He never seemed to be offended by how others treated him. His response to people was always for their benefit. He protected a woman who was caught in the act of committing adultery. On his way to a family whose young daughter had died, he stopped to heal a woman who desperately reached out to touch his cloak as he walked past. He told an unforgettable story about a good Samaritan who cared for a man in need when all others were either too busy or too afraid.

Perhaps most astonishing is the grace Jesus showed as he hung on the cross. He told the remorseful criminal hanging next to him that he would indeed be with Jesus in paradise. This was scandalously unfair. And indescribably gracious. In this same scene, Jesus uttered the famous words,

> *"Father, forgive them, for they do not know what they are doing." —Luke 23:34*

How many times have we been wronged and struggled to show grace? It's possible that people intentionally harm us, but it's unlikely they know how deeply it hurts. More often, we are wounded by people who have no idea they're even wielding a weapon:

- Our parents
- Our co-workers

- Our spouse
- Our church
- Our friends

They do not know what they are doing.

It doesn't take long to discover that Jesus is gracious.

He Is Playful

Jesus is also wonderfully playful. Most of us are consistently attracted to people who make us smile. Few first dates turn into second dates when they are void of laughter. Playfulness is what we often refer to as a "spark."

The Christian *religion* tends to avoid this element. We sing songs with lyrics we don't understand. We lower the timbre of our voices when we read the Holy Scriptures. We must remain somber during Communion and reverent during prayer.

But this joy-starved tone doesn't seem to match the relationship people in the Gospels had with Jesus. Children loved him and wanted to climb up in his lap. Kids don't tend to do that with a thirty-year-old stranger unless he has a warm smile. In the Gospels, we discover Jesus using clever sarcasm, humorous hyperbole, and absurd illustrations.

Luke tells the story of two people who were walking from Jerusalem to a town called Emmaus. It was three days after Jesus died and they were devastated because they had thought Jesus would restore Israel from its six-hundred-year submission to other nations. They were unaware that this was the very first *Easter* Sunday—that Jesus was alive! And he decided to disguise himself before sauntering up to these two people and asking,

> *"What are you discussing together as you walk along?"*
> *—Luke 24:17*

As if he didn't know.

The two people were surprised by the question and asked the stranger if he had heard of the things that happened in Jerusalem. He responded,

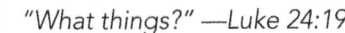

"What things?" —Luke 24:19

Jesus pretended to be ignorant and gave them an opportunity to share what they knew and how they felt. It's possible to read this story with a serious tone, but you would be missing out on his playfulness. Jesus was hiding his identity so he could interact with these people anonymously. He wanted to provide them with an unforgettable memory they could tell their children and their grandchildren. And it's hard to imagine this story being told without a great big smile from the storyteller.

It is natural to believe that the opposite of play is work. We can either choose to be playful, or we can choose to be productive and get something done. Dr. Stuart Brown, president of the National Institute for Play (yes, there is such a thing), says the opposite of play is not work, but depression. We can either enjoy whatever we're doing, or we can remain stuck in a seemingly hopeless rut. Those who forget how to play are more prone to addictions and affairs. We naturally crave excitement, so if we can't find it in a healthy way, we'll search for it in unhealthy ways.

As you spend more time with Jesus, you'll discover that he is refreshingly playful.

These are four attributes of Jesus' personality, and they are all universally attractive. We are naturally drawn to people who are humble, generous, gracious, and playful. There are many reasons to resist the Christian religion, but it's difficult to resist Jesus. These attributes are just a starting point. If you know Jesus, what would you add? If you had the opportunity to spend the afternoon with him, what would you discover?

1. For clarification, the first movie was not originally called *A New Hope*. That title was added later.
2. Philippians 2:8.

3.3 Conflict Stage

Tami and I were admittedly obnoxious when we first got together. From dating to engagement to our first year of marriage, we never had a fight. Really. It was disgusting.

Then we hit year two of marriage and—boom. Our first fight. It was awkward and frightening because it was new territory.

It was just the beginning of many real-life conflicts we have had to navigate. A couple once told me how proud they were that they had never had a fight in their twenty-five years of marriage. That's not something to celebrate. That's an indicator of a major problem. If you're not experiencing conflict, then you're not being honest. A relationship without conflict is like an internal combustion engine without an oil change. It'll run for a while, but it won't take you to all the places you dream of going.

Every real relationship has conflict. If you're in an actual relationship with Jesus, there will be conflict. Are you currently honest about your relationship with him? Do you believe you're allowed to be honest? Has Jesus ever made a promise he didn't seem to keep? Did he promise to be there, but wasn't? Did he promise to provide what you prayed for, but didn't? Does God sometimes seem powerful but not *Emmanuel*? Have you been honest with him?

Sitting on the Hillside

I'm a back-row guy.

If I enter a classroom, seminar, or event, I want to sit in the back row because I want an easy pathway to an exit if things go poorly. I don't want to "Excuse me" my way through a row and announce to everyone that I'm leaving. Some people like to sit in the front—I'm a back-row guy.

I understand the preference to sit on the hillside and listen to Jesus from a distance. It's safer and separates you from those wacky "Christians" who choose to gather at Jesus' feet. You don't need to look into Jesus' eyes, and you get to decide when he's talking to *them* (whoever *them* might be) and when he's talking to *you*. It provides you with an exit if things go poorly.

If you're currently sitting on the hillside, that's terrific. Any time listening to Jesus is time well spent. But you can still experience conflict while sitting on the hillside and keeping your distance because Jesus can be profoundly offensive. For two thousand years, many have struggled with the following words:

> *"I am the way and the truth and the life. No one comes to the Father except through me." —John 14:6*

Jesus' claim of exclusivity is a difficult hurdle for many. Even from a distance, he can create significant conflict—enough that the Jews wanted him crucified and the Romans were compelled to carry it out.

Offensive ideas require two elements: the sender of the offensive idea and a receiver. Occasionally, the sender is offensive—such as someone who utters a racial slur—but an ignorant receiver might not find it offensive. Conversely, a sender might not be offensive—such as an individual who refuses to let his drunk friend drive home—but the receiver is nonetheless offended.

In other words, an idea may not be intrinsically offensive. It depends on both the sender and the receiver. At home, my daughter created an "inappropriate" jar whose purpose is to rid me of one-dollar bills when I say things that she (or Mom) believes are offensive. Sometimes I insert the dollar before I smile and say what I feel needs to be said. Other times I say it, argue about whether it's inappropriate—then insert the dollar.

In the framework of the Overall story that honors Jesus as the crux of the story, Jesus is never offensive.

Jesus, the sender of world-changing ideas throughout his three years of public ministry, is never offensive. If there's any offense, it's on our end as receivers. Why do Jesus' words about money offend us so much? Why do his stories about forgiveness and mercy make us want to pack up our things and leave the hillside? Why do we get so upset in response to his claim to be God?

It's not because he's offensive; it's because we're offended.

Even for those who choose to sit on the hillside, the conflict with Jesus can be very real.

One of the Twelve

It's a different type of conflict, however, when we're connecting with Jesus as one of the Twelve. Eating with him. Walking with him. Sitting in a boat with him.

Jesus grew up near the Sea of Galilee. That's where he chose his twelve buddies and started teaching large crowds. Mark tells the story of Jesus climbing into a boat and crossing the sea with the Twelve.

Years ago, Tami and I got to ride in an old boat across that very sea. The sky was misty, and it blurred the shoreline, making it easy to imagine what it would have looked like two thousand years ago. At one point, the captain shut the engine off and we sat there in the same body of water, looking at the same hills on the shoreline. We could hear "Lord, I Lift Your Name on High" playing through the tiny speakers. I went over to Tami to make a comment about the cheesy worship music from the 1980s. She turned to me with tears in her eyes and said, "I can't sing or I'm going to lose it—it's just too much."

"Me too," I lied.

She's always been more spiritual than me.

The Sea of Galilee is technically a lake, but it's large enough to create massive waves. The captain of our boat said he's seen waves over ten feet high. In Mark's story, a storm came up and tossed crashing waves into the boat. Though four of the Twelve were fishermen, the storm was severe enough that even they were frightened. But Jesus didn't offer much comfort:

> *Jesus was in the stern, sleeping on a cushion. The disciples woke him and said to him, "Teacher, don't you care if we drown?" —Mark 4:38*

Jesus was exhausted from healing people and teaching all day. I wonder how they decided who would wake him.

"John, you do it—you're the 'one Jesus loves.' "

I bet it was Peter.

Have you ever been in a situation like these Twelve? The storm is raging and things are completely out of control. Nothing seems to be going right. You turn to Jesus because you believe you have a relationship with him—and he's sleeping on a cushion. It's reasonable to have the same thought as the disciples: "Don't you care about what's happening to me, Jesus?" We assume Jesus would respond most quickly to those who are closest to him.

If a casual friend called me at work and said, "It's an emergency—I need you to come to my house right now because I can't get Netflix to work," I would roll my eyes and ask him to look up the word *emergency*. But if my wife called with the same concern (and she has), I would reschedule my lunch break and head home as quickly as possible.

We assume the closer we are to Jesus, the more quickly he will show up.

But the opposite is true.

Jesus rushes to those who don't know him:

- He runs to the prodigal son who decides to return home.[1]
- He immediately goes to the home of a family whose daughter is dying.[2]
- He stops and talks with a woman who touches his cloak.[3]
- He leaves the ninety-nine sheep to chase after the one gone astray.[4]

And he rests with those who *do* know him. When messengers informed him that his close friend Lazarus was dying, he told them he would be there in a few days.[5]

A few days.

When the disciples were frightened in the middle of the storm, Jesus rested. For those who don't know Jesus, there is urgency. For those who do know Jesus, there's possibly a need to wait. And remember. And trust.

This is where prayer fits into the story. Those on the hillside may pray to a distant God and wonder if that God ever has time for their seemingly insignificant concerns. They hope God hears them, but they're not sure. Those who are one of the Twelve, however, simply *talk* to Jesus when they pray. They know Jesus is right there with them as promised. They don't need to close their eyes and pray in a specific way using certain religious words. They know they can whisper, and Jesus will hear them. They know they can yell, and Jesus will not abandon them in disgust. They understand that a real relationship always involves communication. As a result, there are celebrations and questions and disappointments. And there is conflict.

Imagine you're one of the Twelve, crossing the Sea of Galilee with Jesus. How does the sky look in your life right now? Is it clear and blue? gray and misty? dark and stormy? Is the sea calm or are the waves raging? What is Jesus doing? Is he rowing or is he sleeping? How do you feel about his role in your life? Is there conflict in your relationship with him right now?

Apathy

Conflict is a good thing because it means you're still engaged. A lack of conflict can mean apathy.

Have you ever experienced the powerless feeling of trying to stay awake at the wheel? You're in a hurry to arrive at your destination. You want to keep going because you don't want to pay for an extra night in a motel. The kids are finally quiet. You want to stay awake, so you roll the window down, turn up the AC, crank up the music, smack yourself in the face, and pinch your leg. It's horrifically dangerous because none of it works.

The smartest thing is to pull over.

At the end of Jesus' three years, on the night he was betrayed, he asked his disciples to keep watch while he took time to pray:

> *Then he returned to his disciples and found them sleeping. "Simon," he said to Peter, "are you asleep? Couldn't you keep watch for one hour? Watch and pray so that you will not fall into temptation. The spirit is willing, but the flesh is weak."*
> *—Mark 14:37–38*

Peter again.

His name was originally Simon, but Jesus changed it to Peter, which means "rock." In this moment, Jesus called him by his old name. I wonder if he was thinking, "I didn't mean 'rock' as in 'sleeps like a…'."

Jesus was not afraid of conflict. Not afraid to challenge people and call them out. The fate of humanity was in the balance, and his closest and most trusted allies had fallen asleep. Jesus was aware of the story on the upper level of the stage. There's a cosmic battle going on around us between the indescribable love of God and the vile hatred of the enemy. There's a battle for your heart and the hearts of your friends and family members. Yet we can become so familiar with the story that we simply and tragically—fall asleep.

This is what I struggle with. I don't tend to be offended by Jesus from a distance or complain to him in the boat. What I tend to do is forget the Overall story and nod off to sleep. I can go weeks, even months, leading a church and talking about Jesus, but essentially doing all of it in my sleep. It's like having a priceless piece of art in the living room, but no longer seeing it or appreciating it. It's like eating the same exquisite meal over and over again until you no longer taste it. It's bland, uninteresting, and unenjoyable.

Jesus went away to pray two more times and came back to find his disciples sleeping both times. They kept driving. They were deeply committed to staying awake and pleasing Jesus, but they were powerless. "The spirit is willing, but the flesh is weak."

Like a tired driver, highly motivated to care for the kids in the back seat, we need to remember what's at stake. What happens to your eternity if you are apathetic toward Jesus? What happens to your family if you don't help them understand the epic story of God? What happens at your church when you don't identify something to passionately participate in? What happens to a nation that believes God's plan for marriage and family is archaic and irrelevant?

The smartest thing is to pull over. Stop the car and be honest about your fatigue and your apathy. What can you do differently that will help wake you up?

Also, be honest about your conflict with Jesus. What part of the Old Testament story doesn't fit well with you? What part of the modern church experience doesn't make sense to you? What circumstances in your life do you need help understanding?

Be honest with Jesus. He can handle it.

Conflict is not bad. It's not an indicator that your relationship with Jesus is a mess; it's evidence that your relationship is real.

1. Luke 15:17–20.
2. Matthew 9:18–19.
3. Matthew 9:20–22.
4. Luke 15:4–7.
5. John 11:1–6.

3.4 Growth Stage

A relationship with Jesus starts with a decision to trust and follow him. We then enter the enjoyable stage of discovery. If one chooses to endure the conflict stage, what is the goal? What is the overall purpose of this unique yet real relationship with a Jewish rabbi from two thousand years ago?

Growth.

Growth is the indicator of life because anything not growing is dying. It's the movement from *A* to *B*. It's the desire to become faster, wiser, stronger, better. To move from less to more, from awful to less awful, from good to great.

Growth is movement, and we all want it. It's why you're reading this book. What would it be like to see the framework of the Overall story so that it can shape how we live our lives? Is it possible to have an active relationship with Jesus of Nazareth? Could that relationship make a positive impact on your life and your relationships?

Information is interesting. We can receive data and increase knowledge on countless topics. I just searched "meaning of life" on Google and gained access to 812 million results in 0.81 seconds. The first one was, of course, Wikipedia's handling of the subject. The second was Monty Python's movie from 1983, but I know not to go there.

Information is intriguing, but what we really desire—is growth. Change. Movement. Fortunately, that's the result of a healthy relationship with Jesus. He doesn't promise happiness, but he does promise growth.

From Lost to Found

The fifteenth chapter of Luke is the chapter of lost things. It's wildly encouraging for all who have felt or feel lost. Jesus first talks about a shepherd with a hundred sheep who leaves the ninety-nine that are stable to pursue the one that is unstable. The shepherd then throws a party:

> *"Rejoice with me; I have found my lost sheep."* —Luke 15:6

Similarly, a woman loses one of her ten coins, then celebrates after she searches her entire house to find it:

> *"Rejoice with me; I have found my lost coin."* —Luke 15:9

Then we have the famous prodigal son story. The youngest son takes an early inheritance and wastes it on small things that seem like important things to the foolish. But he comes to his senses and returns home to a loving and welcoming father, who says,

> *"This son of mine…was lost and is found."* —Luke 15:24

From Blindness to Sight

In another story, Jesus heals a man born blind by spitting in the dirt to create a paste that he puts over the man's eyes. Dirt to paste requires more than a modest spray of saliva. This was a throat-clearing mouthful of moisture—a *holy loogie*. Perhaps Jesus' twelve buddies watched this healing and thought, "No—no—don't put it on his face—yuck!"

In this story, all the witnesses sadly missed the point. The disciples were interested in the theology, wondering whether this man's blindness was caused by his sins or the sins of his parents. The observing neighbors were interested in the details, curious if this really was the blind man from their village. The religious leaders were focused on Old Testament rules, concerned that this so-called healing took place on the Sabbath. Finally, the man's own parents responded out of self-protection, fearful their family would be unwelcome in the synagogue if their son's healing was not copacetic.

The tragedy is that no one celebrated. No one was in awe of the miraculous change from blindness to sight. Looking for an explanation, the neighbors asked, "Where is this man who healed you?"

> *"I don't know," he said.* —John 9:12

As in, "I was *blind*. I didn't see who he was or which direction he came from because I was *blind*!"

The religious leaders prodded him with questions about the character of the healer.

> *He replied, "Whether he is a sinner or not, I don't know. One thing I do know. I was blind but now I see!" —John 9:25*

As in, "I don't know how this works. I don't understand the grand story of human existence. I don't know why I was healed, and others were not. One thing I do know. I was blind but now I see!"

From Death to Life

Growth is what we all desire—movement from *A* to *B*. It was promised through Jesus' words and proven through his death and resurrection.

Jesus had to die. He couldn't just teach brilliantly, love extravagantly, and peacefully fade away like Yoda on Dagobah.[1] He had to continue the story introduced in Parts I and II. We learned in Chapter 2.3 that our sin and brokenness can't go unpunished. God is just and cannot simply say, "Oh, don't worry about it." Somebody must pay.

Jesus had to die. He had to pay the highest penalty, then shock the world by showing up three days later. He had to conquer the ultimate *A*-to-*B* movement so that we could conquer ours.

This is the crux of the story. It's the center point. Everything rises and falls on the historical three days when Jesus went from death to life. In Chapter 1.4 we looked at David's response to his indiscretion with Bathsheba. He responded well, but he was not fully restored. We need Jesus in order to complete the full transformation.

We can be fully found.

We can receive full, not partial, sight.

We can enjoy fullness of life.

> *"The thief comes only to steal and kill and destroy." —John 10:10*

The third character in the story prowls around on the upper level, not wanting *any* of this growth to happen.

> *"I have come that they may have life, and have it to the full."*
> *—John 10:10*

This is symbolized through the practice of baptism, which is a public declaration of the decision to follow Jesus. When we are submerged into the water, it represents death. The person we used to be no longer exists. Coming up out of the water represents new life. It's a symbol of the full restoration Jesus has planned for us—from death to life.

Purpose

There are other phrases: from darkness to light, from grief to joy, from slave to free. If none of these connect with you, here's a non-metaphorical understanding of the growth that happens through relationship with Jesus: "I no longer need ____ because I now have ____."

It's another way of saying "death to life." There's something in my life I'm letting go of, something I no longer need, something I am putting to death. I no longer need fame, approval, safety, wealth, alcohol, happiness. If you have experienced growth in your relationship with Jesus, what was your starting point? If growth is the movement from *A* to *B*, what would you identify as your "A"? What or whom did you have to let go of? If you desire growth, what might you have to release?

The second half of the phrase is the "life" part. It's the *B* part of the movement from *A* to *B*. It's something you now have. It's what happens after we decide to follow Jesus, discover who he is, and get stronger through honest conflict. We now have—purpose. Growth leads to purpose. It leads to a reason to get up in the morning and a perspective that rises above our circumstances, temptations, and struggles. You may prefer a different word for the second blank but, in my experience, "purpose" covers a lot of territory.

During high school and college, I knew what I needed. Her name was Tracy. We were very good friends during that time, which is the worst kind of torture for a guy. I was a new believer, and my conflict with Jesus was that he didn't show her how adorable I was. For seven years, I went through a repeating cycle of enjoying her friendship, wanting more, and getting hurt.

Seven years.

During my final year of college, I had a profound experience with God where he said, "Look at the mountains. I made them. Do you think I lack the power to free you from this repeating cycle? Trust me with every area of your life and I will take you places you have not even imagined." And I chose to trust him. It was an unexplainable miracle in my life. God gave me the gift of purpose and helped me to align my priorities under that purpose. This encounter with God led to a ten-year period of tremendous growth and spiritual strength—a season in my life I refer to as the *great decade*. A completely new issue surfaced after those ten years, but we'll explore that in a later chapter.

Here's another example that uses the "I no longer need ____ because I now have ____" phrase. Recall the story of Shelley and her husband from Chapter 2.4. The most deeply wounding conflict Shelley ever had with Jesus was the destruction of her marriage due to her husband's unfaithfulness. But she grew in her relationship with Jesus and found new strength. She decided, "I no longer need the perfect, successful, exemplary story. I no longer need my husband to break free from his lies, his addiction to alcohol, and his adultery. I *want* it. I want him to be free. But I don't need it because I now have purpose. Our kids still need their mom, and God still has more for me to do. I'm not going to let my husband destroy my life. I'm going to let him decide if he wants to keep up with my growth."

Wonderfully, he did. After many years of deception, he hit his own rock bottom. He let go of powerful addictions in his life and was motivated by his wife's clarity of purpose. It took years of tremendous pain, but they experienced profound growth and are now enjoying a renewed marriage together.

Cost

We desire growth and Jesus promises to provide it, but it will cost us something. This isn't a bait-and-switch. A relationship with Jesus is a real relationship, and all relationships cost us something. Some estimate that a child costs half a million dollars to raise. Tami and I have three of them. Do you know what kind of classic cars I could drive for $1.5 million?

Many brides and grooms get cold feet at their wedding because they're walking through a doorway that locks behind them with the words, "I do." And once that door is closed, it eliminates literally billions of other options. A healthy marriage requires husband and wife to give up preferences and wants daily. All relationships cost us something.

In Chapter 3.1 we identified the problem as *control.* We want it but we can't have it. The solution is to trust Jesus with it. Having a relationship with him means that he is Lord of our lives. He's in charge. He's in control.

As an adjective, the word *overall* means "taken as a whole" or "from end to end." When it is separated into two words, it's a phrase that means "above the whole thing." Jesus is not just to have control over part of our lives. He is Lord *over all.*

Jesus is in control. And it's natural for us to struggle with surrendering that control to him.

If you want something to be remembered, it's wise to repeat it three times. If you say something three times in a row, you will communicate its importance. A declaration made thrice will not be easily forgotten. Jesus said the following about the cost of following him:

> *"Whoever wants to be my disciple must deny themselves and take up their cross daily and follow me." —Luke 9:23*

Let go of your *self.* Let go of your need to compare yourself with others and to be better than them. Let go of filtering opportunities through, "What's in it for me?"

> *"For whoever wants to save their life will lose it, but whoever loses their life for me will save it." —Luke 9:24*

Let go of your *life*. Even if you live one hundred years, it will still be a drop in the ocean of eternity.

> *"What good is it for someone to gain the whole world, and yet lose or forfeit their very self?" —Luke 9:25*

Let go of the *world.* It promises everything but delivers little.

An example of the cost of letting go comes from a furniture store owner known as "Mattress Mack." When Hurricane Harvey inflicted devastating damage on Houston in 2017, the 160,000-square-foot showroom of his furniture store was unaffected because it was in a safe and dry part of the city. Mattress Mack sent his delivery trucks to assist in rescuing people who had lost their homes and provided housing for over three hundred of them in his showroom by letting them sleep on brand new couches and beds. He set out piles of towels and clothes for those in need and had a section designated for dogs and cats.

Dogs, I understand. But cats?

Mattress Mack let go of his entire inventory at great financial loss because he saw the power of purpose. This is the kind of change Jesus inspires us toward. "I no longer need ____ because I now have ____."

A real relationship with Jesus is the center point of the entire story of human existence. Either we are *moving* toward that relationship, like the Old Testament moved toward the New, or we are *considering* a decision to be one of the Twelve, or we are *exploring* what it means to grow as a disciple. The rest of the story, and therefore the rest of this book, is about the last option. What does it look like to thrive in a relationship with Jesus?

1. A surprisingly touching scene in *Star Wars: Return of the Jedi* where we witness the demise of a puppet.

PART IV:
REVOLUTION

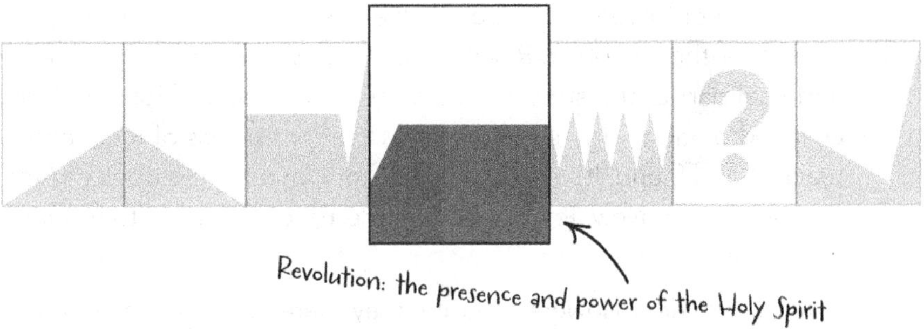
?
Revolution: the presence and power of the Holy Spirit

Intro

Jesus had a succession plan. He poured his life into his twelve imperfect buddies and knew that some of them would be ready to carry on what he started.

What he started was a revolution.

In the Old Testament, the relationship with God grew from the child phase to the teenager phase. Now that we are invited into a real relationship with Jesus, we have graduated into the adult phase. When Jesus asked Levi to become one of the Twelve, Jesus said,

> *"I desire mercy, not sacrifice." —Matthew 9:13*

Jesus was quoting Hosea, one of the Old Testament prophets. At the beginning of the three-year experience with his disciples, Jesus wanted to lay the groundwork for a revolutionary new idea. God wants us to think beyond *my* sacrifices that address *my* sins and restore *my* relationship with God. It's time to think beyond *me*. It's time for the grand story to expand. His people have matured and are now ready to go beyond themselves and beyond their storied nation.

This has always been God's overall plan. We are to get to know Jesus and do what he says. Jesus' overarching message that he left with his disciples was a new marching order that fulfilled all the laws and everything they were taught:

> *"A new command I give you: Love one another. As I have loved you, so you must love one another. By this everyone will know that you are my disciples, if you love one another."*
> *—John 13:34–35*

Jesus started a revolution of love.

This section covers the rest of the New Testament after the Gospels, except for the last book, Revelation, which we'll save for the seventh and final part of the story. It's the story of the young, frightened disciples who had to figure out what to do after the loss of their leader, teacher, and friend. It's essentially the story found in the Book of Acts. The rest of the New Testament is made up of letters written during that period.

Jesus' young followers thought they were disciples of a Jewish rabbi. They didn't know they would become revolutionaries.

4.1 In Jerusalem

Vive la révolution!

The rest of the New Testament story after the Gospels is one of tremendous courage. It's found in the Book of Acts and it's the story of young men and women figuring out how to expand the revolution without the physical presence of their beloved leader. The story covers a thirty-year period, has nearly one hundred characters, and moves through thirty countries and fifty cities, towns, and islands. There are miracles, dramatic escapes, courtroom scenes, rescues, imprisonment, mystery, adventure, and even death. It covers so much territory it could be a James Bond film.

And it's all true.

Napoleon Bonaparte rose to prominence during the French Revolution and is considered one of the greatest military minds of all time. He is credited with the following observation: "Alexander, Caesar, Charlemagne, and I have founded empires. But on what did we rest the creations of our genius? Upon force. Jesus Christ founded his empire on love."

It was a dramatic and courageous revolution of love.

Framework

Part IV of our epic journey has its own internal structure. Bear with me for a moment while I attempt to sketch the framework of the revolution within the framework of the Overall story.

Jesus had one more interaction with his posse before he ascended into heaven. One of those present (hopefully not Peter) asked,

> *"Lord, are you at this time going to restore the kingdom to Israel?" —Acts 1:6*

They still didn't get it. After all Jesus did and said, they still thought it was going to be a revolution that restored earthly power. When my kids were young, I was often surprised at their inability to *get it*. They would ask to watch TV and I would respond, "You know the answer to that question. We just watched a movie before dinner, and I was very clear that we were going to Gramma and Grampa's house immediately after dinner."

They would nod their heads and wait until I was finished talking before asking, "Does that mean we can turn the TV on?"

Sometimes people don't get it no matter how clear we think we are. So Jesus continued his message and offered these final words:

> *"You will receive power when the Holy Spirit comes on you; and you will be my witnesses in Jerusalem, and in all Judea and Samaria, and to the ends of the earth." —Acts 1:8*

This one verse outlines the entire Book of Acts and, therefore, the thirty-year period that makes up the second half of the New Testament. The story takes the form of an ever-widening circle with Jerusalem at the center. The circle expands to Judea and Samaria with the end goal of reaching the ends of the earth. The upcoming four chapters in Part IV (Revolution) will be outlined by Acts 1:8 as well. They will be organized in the following way:

Chapter 4.1: In Jerusalem

Acts 1—7

The revolution builds strength and momentum in the city of Jerusalem.

Chapter 4.2: In All Judea and Samaria

Acts 8—12

The revolution expands to the region of Judea where Jerusalem is located, as well as the region to the north. These are essentially the North and South kingdoms from early in the Violation story.

Chapter 4.3: To the Ends of the Earth

Acts 13—20

The revolution has campaigns that expand to regions around the Mediterranean Sea. This is when the letters titled Thessalonians, Corinthians, Galatians, and Romans were written—all named after the new areas of expansion.

Chapter 4.4: Rome

Acts 21—28

The last chapters in Acts continue "to the ends of the earth" and specifically focus on the most powerful city in the world at the time. It was from a prison in Rome that Philemon, Colossians, Ephesians, and Philippians were written.

I love being able to see the flow of a story. If I get halfway through a movie and can't explain to someone what has happened because it's all too fuzzy, then it's time to find another movie.

Real Time

Back to Jerusalem....

The first thing Jesus wanted for his young revolutionaries was for them to get real. Honest. Genuine. The revolution dies when authenticity dies. I've known many who have decided they want nothing to do with Jesus because of the observed hypocrisy of his followers.

In Acts 1:8 above, Jesus said, "You will be my witnesses." Witnesses of a crime don't need to be experts. They don't need a degree in forensic science. Their job is simply to communicate what they saw and heard. The blind man who was healed by Jesus was questioned about all sorts of details, but all he could genuinely say was, "I don't know. I don't know how it happened. I was blind but now I see."

Witnesses to the love of Jesus don't need to explain difficult passages in the Old Testament or understand why Jesus had to die a gruesome death. They don't need to read an artfully crafted book summarizing the grand Christian narrative.

Ahem.

People aren't interested in your answers; they're interested in your story. They want to know what you have witnessed—what you have seen and heard. It doesn't mean that answers are irrelevant. It means people are rarely "argued" into a relationship with Jesus. Start with your story, then read, study, and grow so you can add theology to it when necessary.

The men and women in the New Testament didn't change the world because they were brilliant theologians, cunning strategists, or gifted orators. Luke, the author of the Book of Acts, describes how people responded to the first revolutionary speech:

> *When they saw the courage of Peter and John and realized that they were unschooled, ordinary men, they were astonished and they took note that these men had been with Jesus. —Acts 4:13*

As Larry Norman wrote years ago, the first followers of Jesus were "unschooled ruffians."[1]

The disciples gained courage and momentum in Jerusalem because they were real. They weren't trying to promote themselves or sell a product. These young revolutionaries shared what they saw and heard during their time with Jesus. And people listened.

Holy Spirit

It was also in Jerusalem where the disciples were formally introduced to the Holy Spirit. Like Jesus, he was there from the very beginning:

> *The earth was formless and empty, darkness was over the surface of the deep, and the Spirit of God was hovering over the waters. —Genesis 1:2*

The Hebrew word for "Spirit" is *ruach*, which is the same word for "breath." As in, "Do not cast me from your presence or take your *ruach* from me,"[2] or, "The *ruach* came into the dry bones and they lived,"[3] or, "My French teacher in middle school had bad *ruach*."

We use the phrase "Don't waste your breath" when we want to help someone and that person is not ready for our help. When a toddler throws a tantrum, it's often best to wait it out. When a drunk friend slobbers "I love you, man," it's probably best to wait until morning to address concerns about that friend's behavior. Don't waste your breath.

When my daughter was little, she wanted us to leave the light on in her room overnight. After I kissed her goodnight, I would say, "Lila, it's nighttime and we have to leave the light off. Are you going to turn on the light again?"

With a smile she would enthusiastically nod her head *Yes!*

I explained, "No, Lila, that's the wrong answer." We would repeat this exchange three or four times until I left the room—so that she could get up and turn the light on. I was wasting my breath.

God doesn't waste his breath. His followers were ready, and it was time for them to be gifted with the Holy Spirit. It was time for them to receive God's *ruach*.

A follower of Jesus isn't just someone who is learning more information than those who are disinterested in the grand story. Followers aren't simply trying to make better life decisions than those who are sitting on the hill listening to Jesus. If you are a follower—a person connected with Jesus as one of the Twelve—then you will experience what the first-century revolutionaries experienced. *You will receive power when the Holy Spirit comes on you.*

Their story is found in the second chapter of Acts. About 120 people gathered to pray and determine next steps. The Holy Spirit entered the room where they had gathered, filled each one of them, and enabled them to speak in other tongues, meaning those around them could understand them even though they spoke different languages. Some thought the whole event was uncivilized and assumed the young followers of Jesus had too much to drink. Peter stood up and addressed the crowd:

> *"Fellow Jews and all of you who live in Jerusalem, let me explain this to you; listen carefully to what I say. These people are not drunk, as you suppose. It's only nine in the morning!"*
> *—Acts 2:14–15*

Peter was the first leader of the revolution—the first pastor in what later became known as the church—and the first thing he said after the coming of the promised Holy Spirit was a joke: "It's only nine in the morning!" If John was on the drum kit, he would have followed up with a "badum-pshh." I love the Bible.

Gifts of the Holy Spirit

The role of the Holy Spirit is a critical one, but it can be divisive. What part of Acts 2 was a unique experience for Jesus' followers on that day, and what part was intended to be our universal experience? Once again, it's essential to be real.

In my early church experience, we didn't talk much about the Holy Spirit. We sang about him and believed in him but didn't spend much time listening to him. My first full-time job as a pastor was at a Vineyard church that had a significantly active and expressive experience with the Holy Spirit. Speaking in tongues, prophetic prayer, words of knowledge—these were all new to me. I was told about a layperson in the church named Tom who could periodically hear the voice of the Holy Spirit. I was good with that. I have a *conscience*. I have felt a nudging to do or not do something.

But Tom was different.

One morning I arrived at my office and felt sick because I had irresponsibly blown off a great friend who was the best man at my wedding. We were to each drive two hours from our homes and meet in the middle at a Frisch's Big Boy restaurant for breakfast at 7 AM. I overslept and was awakened by my friend's phone call at 7:15 AM.

Ouch. A charming joke between friends doesn't pull you out of a moment like that. I felt awful. I was sitting at my desk that morning when Tom, whom I had never met, stood at the doorway to my office. He said, "You know what *integrity* is? Integrity is showing up on time when you say you're going to meet your friend at Frisch's Big Boy at 7 AM."

What did you say?

Tom had no way of knowing my friend or my mistake that morning. Did this really happen? Did Tom provide those exact details? Had I been drinking even though it was only nine in the morning? All I can tell you is what I have seen and heard. During my time at that church,

I decided I was ready and wanted whatever God had for me. On my *belt* of spiritual formation, I wanted whatever *tool* God wanted to offer. If that's speaking in tongues, great. I want to learn more about that. If it's prophetic prayer, terrific. I want to meet with people who believe they have that gift.

The key is to be real. Don't pretend you have tools on your belt that you don't have, and don't evaluate others who don't seem to have the tools you have. The Holy Spirit is God. He is a person who chooses to live inside those who choose to follow Jesus. We can either ignore his presence or seek it, but let's keep it real.

Sobering Reality

Near the end of the story in Jerusalem, a passionate new revolutionary named Stephen was falsely accused of speaking against the Jewish faith. In a manner similar to Jesus, he was seized and brought before the Jewish leadership. In his defense, Stephen took the opportunity to outline God's overall story, which was a courageous and outrageous thing for a non-Jewish person to do in front of highly educated Jewish leaders. They weren't happy about it and chose to stone Stephen to death in accordance with their understanding of Old Testament laws. With one final burst of courage before his death, Stephen said,

> *"Lord, do not hold this sin against them."* —*Acts 7:60*

Tragedy and death tend to sober a person up. This peaceful revolution of love is real. It's not a game. It's not wishful thinking. It's not youthful rebellion. If you're going to pretend you're part of it so you can enjoy all the benefits and avoid all the costs, you will eventually be devastated. Stephen was the first to demonstrate his commitment by giving his life. And he, most definitely, was not the last.

1. From the song "The Outlaw," recorded in 1972. Larry Norman was a groundbreaking Christian songwriter and musician who blazed a trail for Christian rock. On that same 1972 album, he wrote a song that asked, "Why Should the Devil Have All the Good Music?"
2. Psalm 51:11.
3. Ezekiel 37:10.

4.2 In All Judea and Samaria

Many tourists visit the Grand Canyon with a water bottle and a good pair of sandals. They gaze at the enticing trails and foolishly decide they're prepared to make a trip down to the bottom. As a result, the National Park Service has posted a large warning sign as a deterrent to unprepared hikers. It's a drawing of a man on his hands and knees, vomiting onto the trail.

Once you see the image, you can't unsee it.

My friends and I decided to prepare well and make the trip down and back in one day. I mean, how grand can this canyon be? Early in the morning, we began our descent down the South Kaibab Trail. We could see across the entire canyon as well as a little crack down the middle that I assumed was the final drop down to the river.

After two hours of hiking, we arrived at the top of the "little crack." It was enormous. That final drop was larger than what I imagined the entire canyon to be. I was walking alone at this moment, and I teared up as I listened to a majestic worship song from my phone. I was so overwhelmed that my legs were wobbly, and I could barely stand. I didn't have to surrender my man card because, according to Ron Swanson's *Pyramid of Greatness*, crying is acceptable at funerals and at the Grand Canyon.[1]

What I initially thought was a "little crack" turned out to be the steeper, more aggressive second half of the descent. The Grand Canyon is far bigger than I had ever imagined.

Judea and Samaria

We now move into the second section of the story found in Acts. The young revolutionaries were discovering that God's story and plan were bigger than they possibly could have imagined. The story was expanding.

> *"You will be my witnesses in Jerusalem, and in all Judea and Samaria." —Acts 1:8*

Immediately after the stoning of Stephen, Acts 8 begins:

> *On that day a great persecution broke out against the church in Jerusalem, and all except the apostles were scattered throughout Judea and Samaria. —Acts 8:1*

Judea was the region surrounding the city of Jerusalem. Samaria was the region to the north and was inhabited by people the Jews disliked and found inferior. This part of the story is found in Acts 8—12 and introduces the most significant leader of the revolution.

Paul

Paul (originally called Saul) was not a bad dude. It's true that he managed the coats for the people who bludgeoned Stephen to death with stones. It's also true that he was on a rampage to murder or imprison anyone who claimed to follow the heretic named Jesus. But he wasn't a bad dude.

He was simply living out the wrong story.

Paul was extremely confident that he was right. He knew there was one God, and he knew the rules and boundaries provided by that God. These followers of Jesus were breaking those rules, and they needed to be stopped.

Our confidence in our own understanding of the story of human existence doesn't make us correct. Paul was confident he was right until he learned otherwise. He was heading for the city of Damascus in search of more disgraceful followers of Jesus when he was knocked off his horse by a blinding light and heard the voice of Jesus saying,

> *"Why do you persecute me?" —Acts 9:4*

It's very good to be confident in your beliefs. I think Jesus chose Paul for this reason. Jesus wasn't looking for someone who was agreeable. He was looking for someone to lead a revolution—someone who could stand firm against tremendous opposition. I think he looked at this passionate, zealous young man and thought, "That's my guy."

God saw a person who wasn't afraid to step on toes—a man who would challenge the Christian leaders in Jerusalem and speak boldly before any audience he faced. Before the American Revolution, John Adams was frustrated by leaders who would demonstrate passion in meetings but wanted to tone everything down when it was time to send a message to Britain. At one point he shouted, "It's a revolution—we're going to have to offend *somebody*!" Paul understood right away that he was joining a revolution.

He didn't cower when he realized he was wrong. He didn't wallow in the profound error of his ways. He discovered the true story and enthusiastically headed in a new direction. He ended up writing thirteen letters that became nearly half of the New Testament. In those letters, he touched repeatedly on the amazing grace of God. He seems to have understood and received that grace immediately. "Jesus is real. His story and his grace are real. Now, Jesus, what do you want me to do?"

Get to know Jesus, and do what he says.

Paul completed his journey to Damascus and met with a Christian leader named Ananias who must have thought the whole thing was a joke:

> *"I have heard many reports about this man and all the harm he has done to your holy people in Jerusalem." —Acts 9:13*

In other words, "Are you sure you have the right guy?"

Then Jesus communicated his plan to Ananias:

> *"This man is my chosen instrument to proclaim my name to the Gentiles and their kings." —Acts 9:15*

So far, the Overall story has been almost entirely about the Jewish nation growing from childhood into adulthood. But Gentiles are simply non-Jews. Now it was time for the revolution to expand in a dramatic way.

God's story is bigger than you could possibly imagine.

Whenever something gets larger, it's more difficult to keep it together. It's easier to maintain quality in a single restaurant than in an expanding franchise. For this reason, some churchgoers wrestle with church growth because it means their beloved community will become more complicated. This is a theme in Paul's letters: as we expand, as we include other nations with other histories, life among the believers is going to get problematic. So we must pursue unity. We must not fight against ourselves as Jeroboam and Rehoboam from Israel's history did. We must not play soccer like children who steal the ball from their own teammates. We are on the same team, fighting this revolution of love together.

This was Jesus' wish for all of his followers:

> *"My prayer is not for [the twelve disciples] alone. I pray also for those who will believe in me through their message, that all of them may be one, Father, just as you are in me and I am in you." —John 17:20–21*

The first character in the grand story is God. And God is *one*—three persons in one (more about that in Chapter 5.1). You and I are the second character, and Jesus prayed that we, also, would be *one*. We're not supposed to be divided into Jew or Gentile, male or female, poor or rich. We're not supposed to individually oppose the evil work of the third character; we're supposed to do it as *one*. That's why followers of Jesus are referred to as a *family*.[2] We are one family. We are brothers and sisters and wise grandmas and weird uncles. We're not supposed to be divided; we're supposed to be *one*.

Peter

The message of expansion was further emphasized through a vision God gave Peter.

You know Peter. He was the dangerous, "ready, fire, aim" disciple who spoke first and thought second. He was the one Jesus chose to be the leader of his church, but I expect there were times when Jesus shook his head in response to Peter. There's much to love about this guy.

In Acts 10, we find two stories intersecting with each other. The first introduces us to a Gentile soldier named Cornelius who was living north in Samaria. He was wealthy, he was powerful, and he was the enemy because he was a high-ranking Roman soldier. He was everything the tightly knit group of disciples were not. Cornelius knew there was a master designer of life, but he didn't know how to connect with that designer. God spoke to him and instructed him to seek out a man named Peter.

The second story is about a supernatural message God gave Peter:

> *He saw heaven opened and something like a large sheet being let down to earth by its four corners. It contained all kinds of four-footed animals, as well as reptiles and birds. Then a voice told him, "Get up, Peter. Kill and eat." —Acts 10:11–13*

If Peter was a vegetarian, this would have been particularly troubling.

This was a message about food. God had reasons to forbid his people from eating certain foods, but that was all about to change. The message was about food, but it was also about something much more important than food. God told Peter,

> *"Do not call anything impure that God has made clean." —Acts 10:15*

The vision was about people. No longer would there be people on the inside and people on the outside. God was preparing Peter for the Gentile messengers Cornelius had sent. Peter followed them back to Samaria and entered Cornelius's house, which he was not supposed to do under Jewish law because the house was unclean. But remember the vision: "Do not call anything impure that God has made clean."

Peter shared the message of Jesus with Cornelius, his family, and his friends, and they all received the Holy Spirit as the disciples did in Acts 2. As I mentioned in the last chapter, there has been a lot of division in the church regarding the gifts of the Holy Spirit. But the stories in the revolution are quite clear. People heard the voice of the Holy Spirit and had glimpses of the supernatural story in the upper level. They acted on this, and made a huge difference in the lives of others. The Holy Spirit is still alive and still active. Hopefully we're not too "mature and sophisticated" to hear from him.

Peter and Cornelius were attentive, and God used them to profoundly expand the story.

You never know how your smaller story fits in the grand story. All Cornelius knew was that he was to send for some guy named Peter. All Peter knew was that he was now allowed to eat bacon. They had no idea that the intersection of their stories was the beginning of a movement that would eventually spread across the Mediterranean Sea and to the ends of the earth. It's like God is the chess master, moving pieces on a million-by-million chess board. We're invited to play our part, and we have been gifted with free will to decide how to respond. You may never know how your small movement fits in the Overall story.

The Holy Spirit said to Peter,

> *"Three men are looking for you. So get up and go downstairs. Do not hesitate to go with them, for I have sent them."*
> *—Acts 10:19–20*

It would be amazing if God consistently spoke that clearly to us. If I heard an audible voice saying "Get up, go to the freezer, and get some ice cream. Do not hesitate to go, for I have provided multiple flavors," I would faithfully respond every time. Every single time.

The invitation to be part of the story is typically more subtle. In the next chapter, we'll explore what Paul learned about discerning God's plan and our role in it. As you explore the vast and breathtaking Grand Canyon of life, that "little crack" in the distance may end up being the greatest part of the journey. God's story is greater than you could possibly imagine.

1. From *Parks and Recreation*, season 3, episode 1, "Go Big or Go Home."
2. 1 John 3:1–2.

4.3 To the Ends of the Earth

A *campaign* is a series of organized actions that are done for a specific purpose. The third section in the Book of Acts (chapters 13—20) covers three campaigns that are typically referred to as *journeys*. I prefer the term *campaigns* because they were organized actions of substantial length, and their specific purpose was to take the message of Jesus "to the ends of the earth."

These campaigns were long, dangerous, and difficult. On his return trip from his third campaign, Paul said,

> *"And now, compelled by the Spirit, I am going to Jerusalem, not knowing what will happen to me there. I only know that in every city the Holy Spirit warns me that prison and hardships are facing me. However, I consider my life worth nothing to me; my only aim is to finish the race and complete the task the Lord Jesus has given me—the task of testifying to the good news of God's grace." —Acts 20:22–24*

This is the New Testament revolutionary version of a Hunter S. Thompson quote: "Life should not be a journey to the grave with the intention of arriving safely in a pretty and well-preserved body, but rather to skid in broadside in a cloud of smoke, thoroughly used up, totally worn out, and loudly proclaiming 'Wow! What a Ride!' "[1]

Can I hear a Tim Taylor grunt?[2]

First Campaign

Paul left with a man named Barnabas who helped convince the other leaders that Paul was now a legitimate follower of Jesus. Paul's first recorded sermon was given in a Jewish synagogue to an audience of both Jews and Gentiles. In it, he walked through the grand story of God. He started with the Israelites' miraculous escape from Egypt, then the time of the kings and the promise of a coming Savior, and clarified that Jesus is that Savior:

> *"We tell you the good news: What God promised our ancestors he has fulfilled for us, their children, by raising up Jesus." —Acts 13:32–33*

This wasn't an emotional message meant to stir up guilt and shame, nor was it a presentation of empirical evidence. Paul simply told them the story: "This is what happened many years ago, and this is what happened in Jerusalem a few years ago."

If you're a Christian, are you prepared to tell the story? Can you explain the foundation of your faith beyond "I've always gone to church," or "I believe because it's what my parents taught me"? Can you articulate your faith beyond a bumper-sticker message?

Second Campaign

Paul had a different companion for this second campaign. He and a man named Silas took a similar route to that of the first campaign, but headed further west toward the city of Athens. This was Greek territory. Four hundred years earlier, it was home of the greatest philosophers of the time: Socrates, Plato, Aristotle—men who, according to their marble statues, all had creepy eyes with no pupils. They were also brilliant. Athens was a place where wisdom and intellect were of the highest value.

Because Paul was offering a new teaching that the people were unfamiliar with, they were intrigued and invited him to speak at the famous Areopagus, which met on Mars Hill. This was the first-century version of a TED Talk invitation:

> *"People of Athens! I see that in every way you are very religious. For as I walked around and looked carefully at your objects of worship, I even found an altar with this inscription: TO AN UNKNOWN GOD. So you are ignorant of the very thing you worship—and this is what I am going to proclaim to you." —Acts 17:22–23*

He called them ignorant! In Athens!

Yes, God chose Paul for a reason.

Throughout his campaigns, Paul challenged people to think differently. He wanted them to look at the grand story of God that, until recently, had been focused on the Jewish people. How did that story blend with their myths, legends, and beliefs? Did this new teaching about a resurrected Christ sound like a scam? Or was it possible that Paul was providing answers that their way of thinking could not provide?

The expansion of the revolution required people to think differently.

Third Campaign

In the final campaign, we discover a group of people who chose to not think much at all. Paul spent a significant amount of time in the city of Ephesus (in modern-day Turkey), and a riot broke out in response to Paul's actions and teachings:

> *The assembly was in confusion: Some were shouting one thing, some another. Most of the people did not even know why they were there. —Acts 19:32*

Sounds like a rally on a college campus. They were yelling and getting angry, and they didn't even know which side they were on. I smile when I read verses such as that.

The third campaign took a similar route to the second. Paul wanted to visit and encourage the new churches in the cities where he went. It was also on this campaign that Paul wrote some of his most famous letters.

1 and 2 Corinthians

The letters of 1 and 2 Corinthians were written to the church in Corinth, a city Paul visited on both the second and third campaigns. The most well-known portion of these letters is 1 Corinthians 13, which is called the "love chapter" and is often read at weddings. Near the end of that chapter, Paul wrote:

> *When I was a child, I talked like a child, I thought like a child, I reasoned like a child. When I became a man, I put the ways of childhood behind me. —1 Corinthians 13:11*

It is time to reason like an adult. The Old Testament laws were written for the children of Israel who grew into teenagers. Now, with the example of Jesus and the gift of the Holy Spirit, it's time to think like spiritual adults. The irony is that this new way of thinking will appear foolish:

> *For the message of the cross is foolishness to those who are perishing, but to us who are being saved it is the power of God. For it is written:*
>
> *"I will destroy the wisdom of the wise;*
> *the intelligence of the intelligent I will frustrate."*
> *—1 Corinthians 1:18–19*

According to the "wisdom of the wise," sacrifice is foolish. Why would I ever give up something for the sake of someone else's gain? How is it possible to win when I lose? It doesn't make sense.

When I was young, I went to summer camp in central Alberta. Each year we would take a hike down to the Red Deer River and enjoy a few hours of swimming. One time, the river started rising rapidly and we were all told to get out immediately. It was a very difficult swim and one of the kids was struggling to make it to shore. A young counselor dove back into the water and saved the camper, but was swept away by the current. His body was never found.

The story of Jesus inspires us to honor that young man as a hero who saved a child rather than a fool who lost his life. The same can be said about first responders and those who serve in the military. The way of the cross is foolishness to people who only understand self-preservation.

The cross made no sense to the Jewish people because their history was about political and economic power. Their God started and developed a mighty nation through miracles and victories. The weakness, brokenness, and shame of the cross were unfathomable.

The cross also made no sense to the Gentiles (non-Jews). They had little understanding of the Jewish story, so the sacrifice was meaningless. To most of them, Jesus was an extraordinary man who died for no apparent reason.

Through his life and his death, Jesus provided the world with a new way of thinking.

Galatians

Another letter Paul wrote during his third campaign was to the church in Galatia, and it had a similar message. There is a *natural* way of thinking about life and responding to people that Paul referred to as the "acts of the flesh." This is the problem of *control* mentioned back in Chapter 3.1. We want to protect ourselves and we want to get what we want. What happens to me is more important than what happens to you. This includes unwise sexual decisions, uncontrolled anger, and self-destructive envy.[3]

But Jesus offers a different way of thinking that Paul referred to as the "fruit of the Spirit":

> *Love, joy, peace, forbearance, kindness, goodness, faithfulness, gentleness and self-control. Against such things there is no law. —Galatians 5:22–23*

I love that last phrase. If we could simply get these nine things right, there would be no need for any of the hundreds of Old Testament laws. We wouldn't even need a modern judicial system if the whole world surrendered to the revolution of love. People rarely get arrested for kindness[4] or for practicing too much self-control.

There's a *natural* way of doing life—and there's a better way.

Romans

Finally, let's look at Paul's literary masterpiece that he wrote to the Roman believers during his third campaign. Some readers of the letter find it "boring" because there are no stories or pictures. Some pastors have tortured their churches with sixteen- or even thirty-two-week series on it. How a Jewish man who was not one of the original

Twelve could write a theological treatise of Jesus that is still ruthlessly debated and dissected two thousand years later is beyond my ability to comprehend. In this letter, Paul articulated ideas his natural brain should not have understood at the time.

The first eleven chapters outline the problem of sin/control and the solution Jesus offers to that problem. In the first verse of chapter 12, Paul wrote,

> *Therefore, I urge you, brothers and sisters,...*

He reminded them that we are *one*—one family.

> *...in view of God's mercy,...*

In other words, "in view of all I have just explained—in view of the Overall story from Abraham to King David to the resurrected Jesus,...."

> *...offer your bodies as a living sacrifice, holy and pleasing to God—this is your true and proper worship. —Romans 12:1*

Paul was transitioning from belief to behavior. Once you embrace the one, true story and are willing to follow Jesus, this is what you are to do:

> *Do not conform to the pattern of this world, but be transformed by the renewing of your mind. Then you will be able to test and approve what God's will is—his good, pleasing and perfect will. —Romans 12:2*

Just as parents are not supposed to have a favorite child, I don't think we're supposed to have a favorite verse in the Bible. At the risk of offending all the forty-some other authors of the Scriptures, I humbly submit that this verse is my favorite. It sums up all the mistakes I continue to make and what I ultimately long for in life.

Do not conform to the pattern of this world. We tend to view our situation as unique. Of the billions of people who have walked this planet, no one has ever seen and heard exactly what I have. While that is technically true, a counselor or therapist is likely to report that there is nothing new under the sun. The same story repeats itself over and over again, with changed names and altered details.

There are patterns of this world.

Adam and Eve were told they could enjoy anything in the garden of Eden except the fruit from the one tree. How likely was it that all they could think of and all they wanted, at times, was that one fruit? If you're married, do you and your spouse repeatedly fight over the same issues? How is it possible that couples haven't figured those things out after twenty-plus years of marriage? When your anger flares up, is it often triggered by the same buttons? If you have children, have people ever said to you, "Enjoy them now because it goes by so fast"? Of course they have.

Then you feel guilty because the unspoken thought in your head is, "Yeah, but this day cannot go fast enough." Then when your kids all graduate from high school, the first thing you say to that new family down the street is, "Enjoy them now because it goes by so fast."

There are patterns of this world.

There are universal patterns such as the effects of excessive alcohol. Few people wake up after drinking too much and think, "I got a lot done last night. I made some good decisions and helped a lot of people." Sexual freedom also exhibits a universal pattern. Successful and powerful civilizations throughout human history end up pushing sexual boundaries because we don't want to be told what we can and can't do. Paul was writing to citizens in the Roman Empire who were surrounded by profound sexual immorality. It's not a new issue—it's a repeated pattern.

And there are specific patterns in each of our lives. How do you tend to respond when you spend time with a certain group of old friends? How healthy is your decision-making when you spend a lot of time traveling for work? What happens to your heart when your daily social media hours creep up?

There are patterns of this world.

But be transformed by the renewing of your mind. Think differently. We can make the right choice in any given moment, but if our mind has not been transformed, we will quickly revert to the old patterns.

I would like to make healthy eating decisions. I would like to have more energy in my day and more days in my life. But when I stare at a menu in a restaurant, I can't order a $10 salad when a bacon cheeseburger with fries is the same price. My mind can't comprehend that. I think of two cavemen. One goes out and clips a few leaves off bushes, then sprinkles some fancy cheese on top. The other kills a wild boar to get some meat, then takes a slice of it and sizzles it on a grill, then puts it in a bun with a side of crispy potato strips. Which of those two cavemen would you select as tribal leader? Which would be a more desirable choice for an unwed cavewoman? I can order a salad periodically, but my brain is not renewed on this issue.

Think differently.

Think differently about God. Remember that there are two levels of the story and there are heavenly beings fighting on your behalf against a brutal enemy. Remember that God has a plan and has given you free will to decide if you want to be *one of the Twelve* and participate in that plan.

Think differently about yourself. You are never alone, and every decision you make—seen and unseen—matters. You are not a worthless soldier, unknown to the Commander-in-Chief. Every hair on your head is known by a King who values you so highly that he gave his life for you.

Think differently about others. No one is expendable. No one is unworthy. Think about the people inside those vehicles who drive you crazy on your way to work. Is it your place to seek revenge on someone or try to make someone pay a price that is impossible for that person to pay? Is it your place to take advantage of someone who is permitting you to do so?

Think differently about your mistakes, hopes, dreams, future, definition of success.

Then you will be able to test and approve what God's will is—his good, pleasing and perfect will. Thinking differently leads us to what we truly want to know: the will of God. Which school should I attend? Which person should I marry? Which job should I pursue? Perhaps things are not going well and you're looking for a change. Is this the right time? Am I making a change for the right reasons? Those who choose to be *one of the Twelve* tend to believe deeply that God's will is indeed good, pleasing, and perfect. And the pathway to that seemingly elusive will is the renewing of our minds.

How did Paul, the former Christian-killer, come up with this stuff? It's revolutionary, but Paul was not finished yet. He had one more item on his to-do list.

1. Hunter S. Thompson, as quoted at https://www.goodreads.com/quotes/47188-life-should-not-be-a-journey-to-the-grave-with, accessed July 27, 2022.
2. Tim Taylor was the name of Tim Allen's character on the TV show *Home Improvement*. The character personified all that is wonderful and ludicrous about being a manly man.
3. Galatians 5:19–21.
4. There is, however, a terrific story of a woman in Cincinnati in the 1990s who got busted for kindness. She was filling expired parking meters with quarters and was arrested because it was illegal.

4.4 Rome

I understand it is significantly cost-effective for companies to use an automated telephone system to manage customer service calls. What I fail to understand is how many people are actually assisted by being "filtered" through the robotic process. If all I needed were the address or the office hours, I could figure that out without calling. In my experience, I need to get past the filtering system and speak with a real person about ninety-nine percent of the time. And that process is rarely a smooth ride.

Me: Hello, I have a question about an unknown charge on my bill.

Evil Robot: Are you saying you need help setting up your new phone?

Me: No.

Evil Robot: Okay, I will direct your call to technical support.

Me. I said, "No!" All I need is help with an unknown charge on my bill.

Evil Robot: I'm sorry, I cannot understand your response. Please use a short phrase like, "Everything is great" or "I will recommend this company to everyone."

Me (shouting): Talk to a representative—operator—person—human—non-robot—sentient being....

My family knows to stay away from me when I start yelling at my phone. I want to speak to an actual person. If that person can't help, I hope to have access to a supervisor. I would like to talk with someone in charge to increase my chances of addressing my issue. I consider this to be a reasonable request. We all know it's the first thing aliens will say when they land on our planet: "Take me to your leader."

Paul had a grand vision. He wanted to impact the world with the revolutionary love of Jesus. He could continue to travel from one city to the next, but he knew that the greatest way to impact the world was to target the center of power. He convinced Roman authorities to take him to their leader.

All Paul's Roads Led to Rome

It's an outrageous story. Paul returned to Jerusalem after his third campaign to find Jewish leaders who were furious with him for teaching outside the Jewish law and inviting Gentiles into the story. A Roman commander removed Paul from the chaos and stretched him out to be whipped. At that point, I might have yelled, "Okay! No Gentiles! I get it, no Gentiles!" But our courageous revolutionary asked,

> *"Is it legal for you to flog a Roman citizen who hasn't even been found guilty?" —Acts 22:25*

No, it was not. Paul was sent to Felix, the governor of Judea and Samaria. Felix needed to be informed of the situation, so Paul had an opportunity to tell him about Jesus. Felix was so intrigued that he brought his wife to meet with Paul in his cell to learn more. These two were taught by an imprisoned man who ended up writing half of the New Testament.

They must have enjoyed it, because it continued for two years.

Felix was succeeded by Festus, who also needed to get caught up on the situation with Paul. He wanted to send him back to Jerusalem, but Paul said,

> *"I am now standing before Caesar's court, where I ought to be tried. I have not done any wrong to the Jews, as you yourself know very well.... I appeal to Caesar!" —Acts 25:10–11*

Take me to your leader.

Once again, Paul got an opportunity to share the grand Christian story with Festus and a visiting king who was curious about this Paul fellow. At the end of Paul's story of Jesus, the visiting king said,

> *"Do you think that in such a short time you can persuade me to be a Christian?" —Acts 26:28*

Yup. Short time or long, that's the plan. Festus and his friend-king agreed that Paul must get his lifelong wish. They put him and other prisoners on a ship bound for Italy.

Influence

Imagine the audacity of Paul. He was a prisoner on a ship that was having difficulty with strong, uncooperative winds, but he tried to tell the Roman soldier and the captain of the ship what they should do. They didn't listen to Paul, and what happened next can best be described in verse:

The weather started getting rough
The tiny ship was tossed[1]

A storm continued to rage for days. They ran out of food and the crew lost hope, so Paul stepped in to lead and encourage them (have I mentioned that he was a *prisoner* on the vessel?). He told them that God had assured him all would survive if they remained on the ship.

If not for the courage of the fearless crew
The [Alexandrian ship] would be lost
The [Alexandrian ship] would be lost

In one final and harrowing attempt to reach land, they cut the anchors loose and untied the ropes that held the rudders.

The ship set ground on the shore of this uncharted desert isle

All 276 on board survived and made it to the island they later discovered was called Malta. This story makes it clear that influence is not limited by role. It's a healthy desire to have the honor of influencing others—to shape them, lead them, guide them. Paul didn't need a title, and he didn't need an endorsement. All he needed was an opportunity. He believed deeply in the story of Jesus and shared it whenever ears were listening.

Prison Letters

Paul eventually made it to his ultimate destination—the capital city of the most powerful empire in the world. He gained an audience with both Jewish and Roman leaders. He remained in Rome as a prisoner/revolutionary for two years:

> *He proclaimed the kingdom of God and taught about the Lord Jesus Christ—with all boldness and without hindrance!*
> *—Acts 28:31*

Luke was a close friend of Paul's and authored both the third Gospel as well as the Book of Acts. Together, these books are considered a "part I and II" of the entire New Testament story. In Luke 1 and Acts 1, the books are addressed to someone named Theophilus. Some believe they were written as a requirement for Paul's legal case in Rome—a comprehensive history of what happened with Jesus and his followers in Judea. Support for this idea comes from the observation that Roman soldiers are always presented as "good guys" in Luke's accounts.

Regardless, Paul had reached Rome and used his time in prison to write more letters. Ephesians, Philippians, Colossians, and Philemon are considered the *prison letters* for this reason.

It might be helpful to separate the "50s" from the "60s." In the AD 50s (loosely comparable to the 1950s in America), Paul wrote the letters discussed in the previous chapter while he was traveling "to the ends of the earth." It was a time of advancement and development. In the AD 60s (just as loosely comparable to the 1960s in America), Paul was in prison for his radical beliefs and did his best to encourage his fellow Jewish law breakers. Okay, perhaps that's a stretch, but it's a good reminder that these campaigns, prisons, and letters were real and were part of Roman and Jewish history.

It might also be helpful to note the order of the letters in the New Testament because they are not chronological, which can be confusing. The order of books in the New Testament is as follows:

- Four versions of the story of Jesus (the Gospels)
- The Book of Acts
- Paul's letters (in general order from longer to shorter)
- Letters from other authors
- The Book of Revelation (which will be addressed in the final section of this book)

Philippians

One of the *prison letters* was written to a church in the city of Philippi, which Paul visited during both his second and third campaigns. It's a letter referred to as the "letter of joy." From prison Paul wrote,

> *I have learned to be content whatever the circumstances.*
> *—Philippians 4:11*

It's perplexing to hear one of my kids complain about being bored while sitting on a couch in front of a TV with countless shows and movies available for viewing, next to a bookshelf with twenty novels that haven't been read, that shares a wall with the garage containing balls, sticks, bats, and gloves for multiple sports. While, at the same time, my other kids are sitting in another area of the house lamenting their own boredom.

Contentment is about perspective and has little to do with our circumstances.

Often, we're content until we compare ourselves with others. You're happy with your salary until you learn how much Bob makes. How could Bob, the guy with the comb-over, possibly make more than you? You are content with the price you paid for your home until you discover the deal your new neighbor landed. Then you start fantasizing about what you could have done with that extra $15,000, and the contentment fades.

> *I know what it is to be in need, and I know what it is to have plenty. —Philippians 4:12*

Paul certainly did. He was a well-educated, highly respected Jewish leader before he met Jesus. Now, as he wrote these words, he was imprisoned and waiting for the possibility of having an audience with Caesar.

And you and I know both "need" and "plenty" as well. We all have experienced great need at some point in our lives. Need for attention, for resources, for healing, for a job. Need for someone to listen, to care, to help. And we have all had moments of plenty. More time than we expected, more food than we needed, more square footage of living space than required. If you have ever had to decide which television or vehicle to purchase, then you know what it is to have plenty.

The Secret

Paul wrote,

> *I have learned the secret of being content in any and every situation, whether well fed or hungry, whether living in plenty or in want. —Philippians 4:12*

Aren't we all longing for that? Aren't we all searching for that *secret* and hoping it isn't a trite, churchy, meaningless, bumper-sticker promise?

> *I can do all things through Christ who gives me strength. —Philippians 4:13*[2]

How does that sound? Whether you're familiar with this verse or not, is there any chance this secret could lead to unlimited contentment? *I can do all things through Christ who gives me strength.*

Years ago, I ran my first and final marathon. I got swept up with a group of runners who convinced me it would be fun. They were wrong. They knew they were wrong, but they just tried to bring as many people down with them as possible. Our group trained well, and I felt great for the first seventeen miles. I was half running and half dancing as I was waving to the hundreds of fans who had no idea who I was. Then things leveled off for about five miles. Then I hit mile twenty-two and my body said, "I hate you." My muscles had a brief meeting with their union representative and decided to go on strike. I remember reading signs on the side of the road and one said, *I can do all things through Christ who gives me strength.*

I won't mention what I wanted that anonymous fan to do with his sign.

I know the verse well, and I believe in its power to carry us through seemingly impossible moments. Paul's words are a beautiful gift—but there's a catch.

They don't mean I can maintain my first-half pace if I just have enough faith. They don't mean I can date whomever I want, buy whatever I want, and live wherever I want if I tap into Christ's strength in me.

Paul's words mean that we can do anything when we're part of the revolution. When we're loving others as Christ modeled, we will always find contentment. When we're practicing humility, generosity, grace, and playfulness (as we discovered in Chapter 3.2), we will consistently experience joy. When we're living out our life's purpose, whether it is surrounded by need or plenty, we will be content whatever the circumstances.

We can experience consistent and forever joy when we are part of the revolution.

Vive la Révolution!

This French phrase means, "Long live the revolution!"

Yes indeed. Christ taught it and modeled it. The Holy Spirit empowered it. Peter, Paul, and others led it. It has reached the ends of the earth and continues to impact billions worldwide. Jesus did not come here to be nice. He came to start a revolution.

Vive la révolution!

1. These are lyrics from the theme song of *Gilligan's Island*, back when TV sitcoms had wonderfully singable theme songs.
2. From the Berean Study Bible translation. The New International Version (NIV) reads, "I can do all this through him who gives me strength."

PART V:
ANVIL

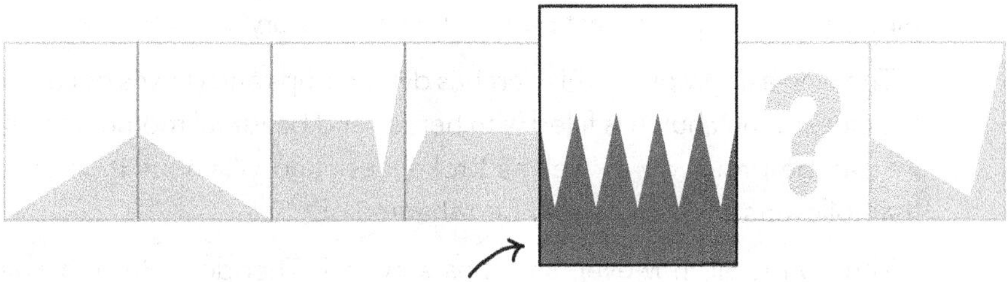

Anvil: the ups and downs of church history

Intro

Imagine entering a conversation and only hearing the last line of a joke. Emma has everyone's attention when she says, "…I don't know, I was trying to send a text message." Ha ha! Everyone laughs hysterically, but you can't even smile because it's not funny. You weren't there. You don't know the story. You don't get it.

Now imagine your sixteen-year-old son pulling your car into the driveway and it's totaled. It's still functioning—he made it home. But every piece of metal on the passenger side is bent, twisted, or ripped apart. How are you supposed to respond? Are you elated because your son seems fine, or are you furious because he was irresponsible? You can't know until you learn the story—until you find out what happened. If he says, "I don't know, I was trying to send a text message," then you'll know exactly how to respond.

We can't understand our present situation without knowing how we got here. We can't figure out how to respond unless we know the back story. There are many terrific resources available in terms of understanding the story in the Bible. There are books, video series, and websites dedicated to the task of telling the story we have looked at so far in this book.

But the story doesn't end with the New Testament revolutionaries. The Overall story didn't pause two thousand years ago. We can't begin to understand what is happening in the world today without exploring the past two millennia.

This section is a ridiculously brief overview of the story of the church. In this format, we can't cover all the essential players and moments. But in the same way that we took a thirty-thousand-foot view of the Bible, we'll explore at least part of the church story.

The *why-axis* graph for this part has dynamic ups and downs because the story of the church is filled with heroes and beautiful moments that we can be proud of, as well as brokenness and villainous moments that followers of Jesus should be ashamed of.

Through it all, however, she[1] has survived. Theodore Beza, a key player in the Protestant Reformation, once wrote, "The Church of God, in whose name I am speaking…is an anvil that has worn out many hammers."[2] Over the next five chapters, we will explore the *Anvil*.

I understand that "church history" is not synonymous with "party time" for most of us. But I'd like to make a deal with you. If you can give this section a try, I will write it without assuming you're interested. In other words, I'll do my best to keep it brief, provocative, and relevant. Can you give it a chance?

Who knows—you may even be pleasantly surprised.

1. Throughout Part V, I will be using female pronouns for the church because Paul (Ephesians 5:25–29) and John, the author of Revelation (Revelation 19:7–9), refer to her as a bride.
2. As quoted at https://www.christianity.com/church/church-history/timeline/1601-1700/beza-last-of-the-great-reformers-11630054.html/, accessed February 2, 2023.

5.1 Theology (AD 50–400)

The word *church* is wrong.

It's somewhat like the word *irregardless*. It's the wrong word, but people keep using it over and over again and we have all just decided to accept it.

Jesus had a plan. He invested in his twelve buddies, knowing that most of them would lead the revolution after he was gone. He specifically called out Peter, whose name in Greek means "rock." He was talking to Peter when he said,

> *"On this rock I will build my church." —Matthew 16:18*

Except that's not what Jesus said.

He said he would build an *ekklésia*, which means "a gathering of people for a specific purpose." It wasn't a religious term. It could refer to any purposeful gathering such as soldiers assembling for war. And the word certainly was not about a building or a location.

As Christian buildings became larger and more opulent, the German word *kirche* was used to describe them. It's pronounced "hchhahkkh" because it's German. And the English word became *church*.

Church is a building. *Ekklésia* is a purposeful gathering. Jesus did not come to build a building. He came to build an *ekklésia*.

The word *church* is wrong, but I'm going to use it irregardless because it's the word we all know. This chapter covers the first few hundred years of her incredible story.

Persecution

Christians sometimes say they want to return to the ways of the early church, or the first-century church, or an Acts-chapter-two church, because we have drifted so far from Jesus' original design. Let's journey back to the first century and explore what that might have been like....

Timothy: Good morning, and welcome to the First Ekklésia of Ephesus. I want to acknowledge Lucius and Cecilia, who are joining us for the first time. Could you please share with the group what brings you here today?

Lucius: Certainly. Our neighbor attends here, and there's something wonderfully different about him, so we wanted to explore who you all are.

Timothy: Terrific! We're glad you're here.

Cecilia: Thank you. I do have a question, if that's okay.

Timothy: Anything.

Cecilia: Why did your people start the great fire in Rome?

Timothy: I'm glad you asked because we didn't. Emperor Nero despises us followers of Jesus. I got a letter from a friend in Rome who believes Nero started the fire himself so that he could rebuild Rome under his own design, then he blamed Christians for the fire.

Lucius: Wow, I had no idea. I also have a question.

Timothy: Fire away. Sorry, bad choice of words.

Lucius: I heard a rumor that you all are cannibals. Is that true? Because my wife and I are definitely not into that.

Timothy: Cannibals?

Lucius: Yes, you drink the blood and eat the flesh of some man named Jesus. I've heard this is one of the reasons the Roman Empire is against you.

Timothy: People fear what they don't understand. It's not cannibalism, it's Communion, and I'm happy to explain that at another time.

Lucius: Great to hear, thanks.

Timothy: Before we get started this morning, I want us to pray for our brothers and sisters in Rome. We know of at least ten people this week who were wrapped in animal skins and torn apart by dogs because they refused to bow down and worship Nero as God.

Lucius: Excuse me?!

Timothy: Yes, it's horrific, but it's better than last week when over thirty were covered in tar, tied to posts on Nero's lawn, and burned alive at night as he hosted guests at his palace.

Cecilia: They didn't do anything wrong? They simply gathered in meetings like this?

Timothy: Yes. Nero is so afraid of us that he has, at times, crucified Christian moms with their babies tied around their necks.

Lucius: I'm going to speak for my wife, whose face is now quite green. We're going to slip out and not return. Why would anyone want to join a group like this—ever?!

Why indeed.

The situation for early Christians remained grim for generations. Thousands were tossed into the Colosseum to be mauled alive by lions and other beasts—all for the pleasure of the Roman elite. The first-century church was bold and courageous, but they experienced unspeakable persecution.

They remained strong and persevered until their world radically changed in AD 313.

Constantine

Emperor Constantine realized that the pesky Christians were not going away. Rome couldn't beat them, so it was time to join them. In the year 313, he legalized Christianity and became a follower of Christ himself. The most powerful person in the world was now part of this underground Christian "cult." It was scandalous.

We can't give too much credit to Constantine, though, because it's possible he made these decisions for political rather than spiritual reasons. I mean, this is the guy who decided Rome was no longer the best city to be the capital of the Empire, so he moved the capital east to the city we now know as Istanbul, Turkey. Istanbul's previous name, however, was Constantinople.[1] He rebuilt the capital city and named it after himself.

Not exactly in line with

> *Humble yourselves before the Lord, and he will lift you up.*
> *—James 4:10*

Nonetheless, AD 313 was a huge deal. It was the beginning of a monumental shift in power that impacted the *Anvil* for centuries, which we will explore in upcoming chapters.

The immediate impact was that Christians were now free to focus on something other than mere survival. They could ask questions and publicly debate differences in ways that were never possible before.

Theology

Theology is the study of God. It means thinking about what you believe before you need to rely on that belief. Much of our current understanding of God was formed by the brilliant and courageous question-askers of the fourth century.

For example, Arius was a follower of Jesus who wanted to understand the relationship between Jesus and God. In Luke's story of Jesus' birth, an angel says the child

> *"...will be called the Son of God." —Luke 1:35*

So Jesus was the offspring of God. He was made *from* God. Created by God. Arius concluded that Jesus was therefore not equal to God. After all, we see in the Gospel stories that Jesus talked to God and prayed to him.

Wait—what?

This view became known as Arianism (not to be confused with Aryanism, which is about racial supremacy and came much later).

A man named Alexander had a different understanding. He asserted that Jesus *was* God. After all, Jesus said

> *"I and the Father are one." —John 10:30*

and

> *"Anyone who has seen me has seen the Father." —John 14:9*

Emperor Constantine called the Council of Nicaea in AD 325 to settle this debate. They met for about a month, sided with Alexander, and created the Nicene Creed. The first few lines of each of the three sections in the creed are:

> We believe in one God,
> the Father, the Almighty,
> maker of heaven and earth....
>
> We believe in one Lord, Jesus Christ,
> the only Son of God,
> eternally begotten of the Father,
> God from God, Light from Light,
> true God from true God,
> begotten, not made....
>
> We believe in the Holy Spirit, the Lord, the giver of life,
> who proceeds from the Father and the Son....

This was an impressive document. In my church, it took us over six months to craft missional language in children's ministry. In Nicaea, they had a month-long gathering of church leaders from multiple regions and produced foundational language that has remained largely untouched for 1,700 years. That's impressive. If you're amazed by the brilliance and insight of America's Declaration of Independence (which you *should* be), then the creation of this ancient theological document should blow you away.

The Trinity

The three sections of the Nicene Creed laid the groundwork for the concept of the *Trinity*.

When I was in college, I visited a ministry that met on campus. The first time I went, a well-intentioned, awkward young man named D'arcy welcomed me with a barrage of questions. I remember his name because it was spelled D'arcy.

"Do you believe Jesus is the Messiah?"

"I think so." I was studying engineering at the time. I was years away from my attempts in seminary to study theology.

"Do you believe in the virgin birth?"

"I think so." That's the Christmas story, right?

"Do you believe in the resurrection?"

"I think so." That sounds really important.

"Do you believe in the Trinity?"

What a relief. I knew the answer to this one. "Yes, I like all the Star Wars movies."

I had no idea what a Trinity was, and now, decades later, it remains a mystery. The word *Trinity* is not found in the Bible. It's a way to capture the beautiful mystery that the Father, the Son, and the Holy Spirit are three distinct persons, yet together they are one. Explaining the Trinity is like an ant trying to describe the Internet to another ant. The best attempt I've seen is a diagram created a thousand years ago called the "Shield of the Trinity":

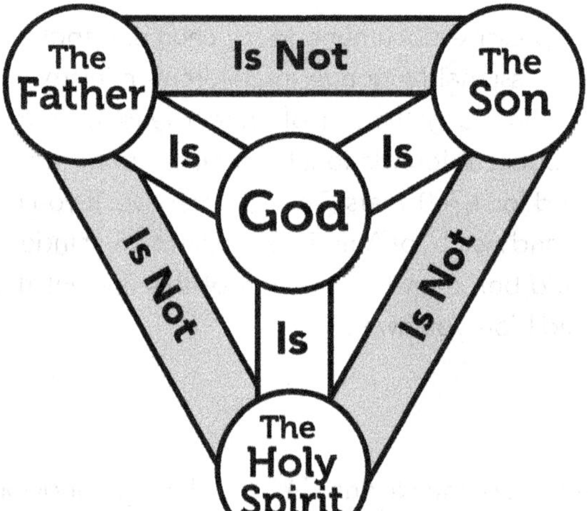

God is one—there are not three gods. The Father, the Son, and the Holy Spirit are all God, yet they are *not* one another.

Can you hear the ant saying, "Okay, there's this thing called electricity..."?

Human Made

Theology is great. This book you hold in your hand is *theology*. I don't tend to use that word because it sounds more sophisticated than anything I would write. I prefer to talk about the spectacular story of God. But it's all theology.

Theology is great. But it's a human endeavor.

The Bible, on the other hand, is the protected Word of God. It has its own story of development that involved imperfect people making decisions about which writings and letters made it into the Bible and which did not. But it's protected by God:

> *All Scripture is God-breathed and is useful for teaching, rebuking, correcting and training in righteousness.*
> *—2 Timothy 3:16*

The Bible is the breath of God. It is the only tangible, readable item God has given us in order to understand him and his story. Everything else is human made.

For this reason, theology should always be approached with humility and grace. Some ideas, such as the Trinity, have stood the test of time and deserve to be held rather tightly. Other ideas may be new, provocative, and enticing. Explore them, including anything written in this book, but remember they are all human made. They are simply an attempt to understand the grand, God-made story.

Besides, the *Anvil* didn't survive the first few centuries because of theology. Theology doesn't transform hearts. The church survived because it embraced the mandate from Jesus to "love one another." In the face of horrific persecution, early believers continued to care for the sick, the orphans, and the elderly. They honored families by taking care of dead bodies that were littering the overcrowded streets of the big cities. They loved and loved and loved. And after 250 years, Roman leaders finally took notice.

The Roman Empire has come and gone. But these poor, broken, scared groups of Christians met in secret as God's *ekklésia* and are now billions strong.

Love won.

---

1. If you know the 1990 song by *They Might Be Giants* (or the 1987 version, or the 1976 version, or the 1953 version), then I'd be surprised if the chorus was not playing in your mind as you continued to read. My apologies.

5.2 Darkness (AD 400–1500)

Vincent Price hauntingly begins the spoken-word section of Michael Jackson's song "Thriller" with the words, "Darkness falls across the land." Please refrain from doing the zombie dance move and stay with me.

These words are a fitting introduction to the next eleven centuries of the church story. There were bright moments and faithful followers who held the church up during this time. Saint Francis of Assisi was a beloved monk who wrote, "Lord, make me an instrument of your peace." John Wycliffe translated the Bible so regular people, not just the educated clergy, could read it. But this lengthy period of history—not just church history—is referred to as the *Dark Ages* for a reason. The church drifted far away from the light—from the message of Jesus—and entered the darkness. There were two movements of the church during this time that are difficult to imagine and painful to accept. But just like our own life story, it's not helpful to pretend the nasty stuff isn't there.

Hang in there, though, because this journey through darkness will lead us to a very important question.

The Crusades

The first movement was a series of religious wars known as the Crusades.

By the year 400, the sacred city of Jerusalem had faded into the background. Jewish people weren't there because they were kicked out by the Romans. Christians weren't there because their center of power shifted to Rome and remained there through the Dark Ages. The Temple Mount—the place where Solomon's temple was built, the place where Jesus learned as a boy and taught as a man, the most sacred piece of dirt on the planet—became a literal garbage dump.

The Christian story moved west, while in the east there was tremendous poverty, unrest, and death in the region called Arabia (now known as Saudi Arabia). In the city of Mecca, a man reportedly was visited by an angel and received a calling to lead his people out of misery. His name was Muhammad,[1] and he put together the book known as the Qur'an[2] and founded Islam. He brought the people of Arabia together and led them to become a powerful nation, united as followers of Allah.

In AD 637 they expanded to Jerusalem, overtook the city, and built a Muslim mosque in the center of the Temple Mount. It's called the Dome of the Rock and remains one of the most iconic structures in Jerusalem today.

All was well for hundreds of years until the eleventh century, when Christians in the west decided to take Jerusalem back. The Pope promised both earthly and eternal benefits to impoverished westerners and built an army of thousands. They marched to the city, slaughtered Muslims, and took control of Jerusalem. The motto of the Christians was, "Kill them all and let God sort it out." Then they lost the city back to the Muslims. Then they recaptured it. Then they lost it again. These religious wars, that remain an embarrassingly dark part of church history, are known as the Crusades.

For a thousand years, Christians believed they had the one, true story, as evidenced by the fact that people in every generation were willing to die for their Christian faith. But through the Crusades, they learned something shocking about the Muslims: they also believed *they* had the one, true story, as evidenced by the fact that people in every generation were willing to die for their Muslim faith.

If both groups were willing to die for their faith, how do we know which one is right?

It's important to understand that Muslims believe much of what Christians believe. They believe in Adam, Noah, Abraham, and Moses. They even believe in Jesus, but they think he was a prophet, not God. As noted in the following chart, Islam grew out of the Jewish and Christian stories:

Phase	Beginning	World Religion	Book	Central Figure
I	1500 BC	Judaism	Old Testament	Moses
II	AD 30	Christianity	New Testament	Jesus
III	AD 622	Islam	Qur'an	Muhammad

Judaism (the story in the Old Testament) set the stage for Christianity in similar fashion to the way both Judaism and Christianity set the stage for Islam. Jewish people believe Phase I of the story and stop there. Christians believe Phases I and II. And Muslims believe all three and that the Qur'an is the full and final revelation of God.

Four thousand years of history and it comes down to a rant between Lloyd and Harry:

> Lloyd (Muslims): "Triple stamped it, no erasies, touch blue, make it true."
>
> Harry (Christians): "You can't triple stamp a double stamp! You can't triple stamp a double stamp!"[3]

Pause there. We'll come back to this in a moment.

Inquisitions

As the darkness of the Crusades was starting to fade, the church entered a new horrific season known as the Inquisitions.

Christianity was expanding into new areas of Europe, and without the printing press or any method of mass communication it was difficult to keep everyone on the same page (so to speak). The Pope at this time had tremendous spiritual and political power and wanted to control the spiritual growth of the people spread out across Europe. His plan was to officially grant church leaders power to use torture to force confessions out of non-believers. The idea was that it was better to suffer now and experience peace in eternity than to experience peace now and suffer in eternity. It was somewhat of a *Thanos* argument from Marvel fame, whose approach was essentially, "I'm doing this despicable thing for your own good."

Men, women, the elderly, and even children were tortured until they professed Jesus as Lord. It's unfathomable.

The name of the Pope who initiated this nonsense was Pope *Innocent* IV. I can't make this stuff up.

The church wandered around in the darkness for so long that she forgot the beauty and power of the Light. The string on the bow pulled back tighter and tighter through these centuries, and it's no surprise that something had to give. The next chapter is the story of that exploding arrow.

A Very Important Question

Before we move on, I want to bring a very important question to the surface. The question is for *thinkers* who want to study the information and choose the logical pathway. And it's for *feelers* who want to have profound experiences and don't feel the need to explain them. The question is this: *What story do you believe you're living in?*

I shared in Chapter 3.1 that my driving question that led me to fully choose Jesus was, "If you grew up across the street from a Muslim mosque, would you be Muslim?" At the time, I had no idea how Judaism, Christianity, and Islam were related. All I knew was that I had to choose something. I had to decide what was the one, true story of human existence. It was a hugely important question a thousand years ago and it remains so today: *What story do you believe you're living in?*

Since you're reading this book, it's likely you have chosen the Jesus story. But here's a four-step process for those who don't yet know their answer to this question.

Step One: Design vs. Chance

This is the beginning of the faith conversation. A person must decide if there is an intelligent designer of the universe and life on this planet. Are the unique properties of water, the mating dances of manakin birds, and the ability of the human eye to transform light into images the work of design or the result of evolutionary chance? Those who believe everything formed by chance will live in that story. Those who believe in design proceed to the next step.

Step Two: *Major vs. Minor*

After officiating a funeral one time, I drove with the funeral director to the gravesite. He said, "Spiritual leaders come in to do their little speeches all the time when people die, and they are so ignorant."

I thought, "No offense, in case you were wondering."

"Every faith system says the same thing," he continued, " 'Peace, love, hope, remember and celebrate the lost....' They all have a different name for God but it's all the same thing. I have no patience for such ignorance."

They're not all the same. Step Two separates the major religions from the minor. Thousands of attempts have been made to explain the miraculous design of life. There are a variety of cults, alien-inspired religions, crystals in Sedona, the Temple of the Jedi Order....

Yup.

These are minor religions as opposed to the five major ones that have stood the test of time: Hinduism, Buddhism, Judaism, Christianity, and Islam. While it's true that being popular and widespread doesn't make something right (look at the *Macarena* from the 1990s), there is tremendous credibility to faith systems that have survived centuries of scrutiny. Those who are drawn to a minor religion will live in that story. Those who trust one of the big five, proceed to the next step.

Step Three: *West vs. East*

Judaism, Christianity, and Islam are considered western religions, whereas Hinduism and Buddhism are eastern. The eastern religions are connected in that they both originate from India, with Buddhism descending from Hinduism. Both believe in a life-force that sustains the universe and refer to it as *karma*. All three western religions believe there is one, almighty God, whereas Hinduism believes in hundreds of gods and Buddhism believes there is no god. Those who believe there is one God, proceed to the final step.

Step Four: the Big Three

Why Jesus? In the Judaism-Christianity-Islam table, how do we know Jesus is the crux of the story? There's a tendency to respond with a *churchy* answer, which is something that is true, but we either don't know what it means or we don't think about the meaning when we say it. A *churchy* answer is something we only say in church, such as:

- Jesus died on the cross for my sins.
- Jesus washed me with his blood.
- I am a born-again believer.
- If the service at a restaurant is bad, I don't tip (bad joke, sorry).

So how does one choose? It's uncommon to deeply explore Judaism, Christianity, and Islam. I'm typically not impressed with those who say they have "studied world religions"—especially if the one making the declaration is nineteen years old. Some people spend their whole lives studying one book of the Bible. Reading *Wikipedia* articles does not constitute "studied world religions."

I'm not a Christian because I dismantled everything else. I'm a Christian because I believe this is the true story. I'm a Christian because I believe there's one, true God who created all things and wants a relationship with me. If God doesn't care about me, then I'm not concerned about pleasing him. As amazing as Wayne Gretzky is, I don't have a relationship with him (yet), so I don't care what he thinks of me. It's all about relationship.

Judaism is about the rules. Islam is about the Five Pillars. Christianity is the only major faith system that is based on a relationship with God. That story makes sense to me, so that's the story I am living in.

The Story Matters

What story do you believe you're living in?

This is an extremely important question because it shapes how we live our lives.

One morning I was running in my neighborhood, and I saw a couple I had not seen in church for a while. They had that "oh-no-there's-the-pastor" look on their faces, so I made sure to go over and say "Hi." They had been trying to have a baby and, about a year earlier, experienced the agony of a miscarriage. A well-meaning person at our church told them, "It's God's will. You just have to have faith and keep praying."

Let me just say: please don't say things like that. It's worse than *churchy* language because it's not true. It's not God's will that a baby dies. Ever. God doesn't make terrible things happen. He weeps at our pain, loss, and suffering. He doesn't *cause* pain—he redeems it. The church is an *Anvil*. It's supposed to *take* hits, not deliver them.

This wounded couple came to believe they were living in a story with an unloving God. They decided not to be hypocrites and continue coming to church when they no longer believed in the story.

The story you believe you're living in shapes how you live your life.

If you don't connect with the story we have explored so far in this book, what story do you believe? If the story of Jesus doesn't make sense, what's the alternative? What gives you peace on days when the world seems to be falling apart? In what do you trust? Faith doesn't change our circumstances—it teaches us how to respond to them.

The point is not to combat those who believe differently, as they did during the Crusades. Muslims were not and are not the enemy. They simply believe in a different Overall story, and that story shapes how they live their lives. The point is not to force anyone to confess Jesus as Lord, as they did during the Inquisitions. Those victims were shaped by a story of oppression, not invited into a story of a loving relationship with Jesus.

The story of Jesus is the one, true story. It's the story that brings light into our darkness.

---

1. His name was originally an Arabic name and there is no literal English version. For this reason, the name can be spelled numerous different ways: Muhammad, Mohammad, Muhammed, Mohammed, etc.
2. There are similar issues with the word *Qur'an*, which can also be spelled *Quran* or *Koran*.
3. This is a reference to a scene in the movie *Dumb and Dumber*. If you dislike the movie, it's probably best if you simply move on and accept my apologies. If you're unfamiliar with the movie, perhaps you should watch it and see the "obvious" connections with church history for yourself. If you are a fan of the movie, you're welcome.

5.3 Reformation (AD 1500–1600)

Leadership and authority have been significant issues in the story of the church. One of the early influences for me as a pastor was the annual Global Leadership Summit in Chicago where Bill Hybels repeatedly and passionately taught thousands that "everything rises and falls on leadership."

In 2018, Hybels retired early because of allegations of sexual misconduct, and the amazing church that he founded and led for forty-three years went through a painful season of loss and confusion. Hybels's journey as their pastor was an accurate reflection of his leadership message: Everything rises and falls on leadership.

Leadership is one of the main reasons people love their church. People love to be led in worship by profoundly gifted singers and musicians. They appreciate sitting and listening to excellent communicators who have prepared well for the Sunday message. They look forward to their midweek small group when it is led by someone who is wise, experienced, and compassionate.

Leadership is also one of the main reasons people dislike the church. The media pounces on any juicy story of a church leader having a moral failure. Critics have seemingly unlimited stories to support their "anti-church" perspective. Anyone who has experienced a church leadership fiasco as a staff member, leader, or attendee knows the deep-rooted pain and suffering it can cause.

Is the church supposed to have bigger-than-life, superstar leaders who are profoundly talented and influential? Or is this too much weight and pressure for human beings to handle? Should the church focus more on shared leadership and dialogue rather than one overall leader? Should the church embrace messy authenticity more than high quality and savvy strategy? Is traditional leadership the most powerful and effective approach so long as the leader is healthy, accountable to others, and surrendered to Christ?

Our confusion on the topic of church leadership is not new.

Letters from Earl

I am honored and excited to introduce, for the first time, an incredible and authentic historical document (no, it's not). These are actual letters (totally made up) from an English student named Earl to his parents (not real) about his education at the University of Wittenberg in Germany, beginning in 1517.

September 6, 1517

> Dear parents, I made it safely to Germany and finished my first week of classes. I love you both but I'm still very upset that you sent me to this pathetic new school. The professor of biblical studies is a mousy man named Dr. Martin Luther. He's awkward, clumsy, and obsessed with his own sin. He has a hard time making it through class without running to the altar to repent. I can't imagine this guy making a difference in my life or anyone else's. Love, Earl.

October 15, 1517

> I can't stand Dr. Luther. I'm working incredibly hard and I'm barely passing. Mark my words—there will be a glorious day in the future when regular people who are average students in biblical studies can still author a book about our gracious God. We did get some comic relief today, though. Dr. Luther was challenging a girl in our class for some obviously poor choices she's been making. She looked him straight in the eye and said, "You can't tell me what is right and wrong. My parents paid extra money to the church so I could have this letter of indulgence from the priest. I can do whatever I want." I thought Dr. Luther was going to explode! His face got red, and he started shaking. My roommate says he's just a *sauer-kraut*, but I don't know what that means. Auf wiedersehen.

October 31, 1517

Hold everything! You will *never* guess what happened today! Dr. Luther went to the front door of the campus church here in Wittenberg and nailed up what he called his *95 Theses*. It's ninety-five challenges to the Pope and the leadership of the church! Things such as "The Pope can't forgive sins," "The church has misunderstood purgatory," "The church can't sell indulgences to get people out of purgatory," and "People can't buy their way out of sin." It's chaos here! Everybody's talking about it! They're gonna print thousands of copies and distribute them throughout Europe! I think Dr. Luther might lose his job over this.

March 15, 1518

Hello parents, sorry it's been so long since I have written. I know you were concerned about me heading off to college and drinking too much wine. Don't worry, I'm not drinking any. They have this new thing here in Germany called "beer" and everyone on campus seems to be enjoying it. I can't imagine it ever being a problem. Anyway, it's been strange to be at the center of history. Dr. Luther shared with us that he never intended to *reform* the church. He loves the church. He just wanted to challenge the authority and leadership. But the more opposition he experiences, the stronger he seems to get. Now it looks like he's gonna go up against the Pope himself! I love this guy. Speaking of authority—how are things going with our gluttonous King Henry VIII? Has Catherine given him a baby boy yet? With love, Earl.

November 23, 1520

Dr. Luther will soon stand before the most powerful men in the land. They want him to recant what he has written, but there's no way he'll do that. I want you both to know that I'm all in. There's a group of us who are protesting the church's treatment of Luther, which is why some are calling it the *Protest*ant Reformation. I'll keep you informed, Earl.

January 3, 1521

It's done. Dr. Luther refused to recant and was excommunicated by the Pope. I've heard there's a team of people who took him to a castle for his safety, and he plans on translating the whole Bible into German. Some of us followers are jokingly calling ourselves *Lutherans*. I think it's a dumb name and it'll never stick. Besides, "mousy" Dr. Luther would hate it if we used his name like that. What a ride it's been. I'm so glad I made the decision to attend this great university!

Thousands of New Stories

Martin Luther was the reluctant revolutionary credited with starting the Reformation. He was asking the right questions and he did it in an honoring way, but it led to a landslide of division within the church. He inspired other Christian thinkers to lead movements based on issues such as infant baptism, free will, church governance, women in ministry, gifts of the Holy Spirit, and styles of worship—issues that remain dividing points today. The Reformation led to tens, hundreds, even thousands of new alterations of the story of God. It was no longer just the Christian story in comparison to the Jewish or Muslim story. It was now the Lutheran story versus the Reformed story, the Episcopalian story, the Baptist story, etc.

The main separation became Catholic versus Protestant. It's important to understand that the Catholic story was the *only* Christian story until 1517 (except for the Eastern Orthodox Church that separated in the eleventh century). I've heard people say, "I was Catholic, now I'm a Christian." That doesn't make any sense. It would be like saying, "I was a Texan, now I'm an American."

There are significant differences, such as the ways *authority* and *tradition* are understood in Catholic churches versus Protestant churches. In the end, the Catholic Church has some superficial, hypocritical, ignorant church-attenders who have no real relationship with Jesus, and also some Spirit-filled Christ-followers who are passionate about making a difference in the world. And the same exact thing can be said about Protestant churches. The best thing we can do is sit down with Catholics, or Baptists, or Texans and ask what they believe. Focus less on the name of the church and more on the status of people's relationship with Jesus.

The Church of England

One of Earl's letters above mentions the king in England. It's fascinating how the authority of King Henry VIII responded to the authority of the Pope in Rome.

At first, Henry VIII condemned Martin Luther and was honored by the Pope with the title "Defender of the Faith." The king had a daughter named Mary, but his wife, Catherine, was not able to provide him with a male heir. He annulled his marriage of twenty-four years so that he could marry the young and beautiful Anne Boleyn.

The Catholic Church would not support the annulment, so the king said to himself, "I'm Henry VIII I am—Henry VIII I am, I am," and he launched his own church that became the Church of England, with himself as the supreme head of the church.

Did you catch that? He was supportive of Catholic Church leadership until they could no longer provide him with the answers he wanted. Henry VIII's problem, like yours and mine, was one of control. He took his ball and went to play his own game (so to speak).

In 1553, Mary I, the only surviving child of Henry VIII's marriage to Catherine, became queen for five years until she died. Queen Mary wanted to restore connections with the Catholic Church and had over two hundred Christian reformers burned at the stake for opposing her. For this reason, she is known as "Bloody Mary."

Henry VIII and Anne Boleyn had only one child who survived—and it wasn't a boy. It was a girl named Elizabeth. She was queen for the second half of the sixteenth century, and her reign is known as the very successful "Elizabethan era."

Oh, those English.

Pontius Pilate

The Protestant Reformation was a painful but necessary challenge of authority. It's unlikely Jesus would have been surprised by this season in the church's story because he saw such conflict firsthand in the week before his death on the cross.

Let me jump back 1,500 years to the climax of Jesus' story. At the time of Jesus' trial, the governor of Judea was Pontius Pilate. He disliked the Jews because they were pompous and acted like *they* were in charge. The Jews disliked Pilate because he actually *was* in charge, and they hated having to ask him for a favor. They brought Jesus to Pilate in the middle of the night and woke him up. They refused to go into the palace and forced Pilate to come out instead.

A little bit of a power move.

Eventually, Jesus stood alone against the governor. A clash of titans. They talked about leadership. Pilate asked,

> *"Are you the king of the Jews?" —John 18:33*

And Jesus said,

> *"My kingdom is not of this world." —John 18:36*

Pilate was amazed that Jesus didn't beg for his life as others would do. He was intrigued, but he found no reason to crucify Jesus. He told the people gathered outside his palace that he had the authority to release one of the prisoners. The crowd cheered for him to release Barabbas, a known criminal, and crucify Jesus. The soldiers put a purple robe on Jesus and a crown of thorns on his head, mocking him as the "king of the Jews."

Pilate grew cosmically uncomfortable. He knew he was trapped between his emperor, who would not tolerate challenges to leadership, and a mob of unreasonable Jews he didn't want to please.

> *"Where do you come from?" he asked Jesus, but Jesus gave him no answer. "Do you refuse to speak to me?" Pilate said. "Don't you realize I have power either to free you or to crucify you?" —John 19:9–10*

Amazing. He stood before Jesus and said, "Do you know who I am? I'm the one with authority here! I'm the one in charge!" Jesus, with bruises from the beatings and blood dripping down his face, replied,

> *"You would have no power over me if it were not given to you from above." —John 19:11*

Pilate, you are not as powerful as you think you are. You are not the ultimate authority here.

Your Call

Authority, leadership, accountability, structure—these are great things. God trusts us with the keys to the car. We can go explore, have an adventure, try new things. Any victory in the story of the church has required a leader to have a vision and gather people to accomplish something significant. We all have our sphere of influence in which God wants us to thrive. We've been given the keys, but the car is still his. We are not as powerful as we think.

Sometimes we stand before Jesus and say, "Do you know who I am?"

- "I'm the pastor of a large church that reaches thousands of people!"
- "I'm the owner of a company I started from nothing!"
- "I manage a team of people and we are the most effective team in the entire organization!"
- "I'm the parent of three kids, and none of them are in prison!"
- "I'm Henry VIII I am, I am!"

We never say those words out loud, but that's sometimes how we feel. Other people should not be in control because they can't handle it. I, on the other hand, should be given all the keys to the kingdom.

Just like Pilate, Jesus won't cut us off and say, "Quiet, you knucklehead. You are not in charge here. I am the King and you will do what I say." Instead, he looks into our eyes, with blood dripping down his face, and says, "It's your call. You can either try to maintain control or hand it over to me."

You can enjoy your sphere of influence with humility and let Jesus be the King. Or you can walk past him, sit on the throne, claim authority—and see what happens.

It's your call.

5.4 Science (AD 1600–1900)

For some, the Christian story is nonsense.

Are we supposed to shut off our brains and accept ancient ideas about the world that science has proven to be wrong?

During a dinner conversation, Martin Luther apparently talked about a new astronomer who was making the preposterous claim that the earth revolved around the sun. Luther remarked,

> So it goes now. Whoever wants to be clever must agree with nothing that others esteem. He must do something of his own. This is what that fellow does who wishes to turn the whole of astronomy upside down. Even in these things that are thrown into disorder I believe the Holy Scriptures, for Joshua commanded the sun to stand still, and not the earth.[1]

Luther was referring to Copernicus, who was a highly educated leader in the church. Decades later, Galileo, who was also a solid believer in the Christian story, supported the observations of Copernicus. Because this new idea did not seem to line up with some verses in the Old Testament, the church considered Galileo a fool and branded him a heretic.

Moments such as this are part of the church story and are often referenced in conversations about the relationship between science and faith. As science was emerging in the human story, it made elements of faith look foolish. And the debate has continued for the past five hundred years: what is the relationship between science and faith?

Science versus Faith

Why was Martin Luther quoted as an authority on the topic of astronomy? As a pastor, I get very few calls from physicians asking me for my opinion on a medical diagnosis.

In the early 1600s, there was essentially no such thing as *science*. It wasn't even a field of study. In the human story thus far, the greatest thinkers and the most educated were philosophers and theologians. The highest level of study was theology, and everything else fell under that.

Between 1600 and 1900, there was a dramatic shift in the role of science. This period is referred to as the *Age of Enlightenment*, during which René Descartes declared "I think, therefore I am," and Emmanuel Kant wrote that people were finally free to use their own intelligence. It was a time when people boldly began to ask any question and passionately pursue the answers.

In the 1600s and 1700s, physical sciences came to the fore. Galileo provided astronomical evidence that the universe was not what we imagined. Sir Isaac Newton formulated the three laws of motion that we all enjoyed learning in high school. Something about when my body is at rest it should stay at rest? Highly educated in theology, it was never Newton's intention to pit science against his faith. His *laws* were always rooted in the idea of intelligent design. There are laws because there is a lawgiver.

In the 1800s, there was an expansion to the biological sciences. Charles Darwin's theory of evolution was introduced through his book *On the Origin of Species*, and the position of the church regarding creation has been challenged ever since. The tension between science and faith grew with Karl Marx's ideas in social sciences. He went after faith directly through his famous line, "Religion is the opium of the people." He viewed the church as a drug that was sedating people from engaging in thought about the world around them. At the end of the century, Sigmund Freud added behavioral sciences to the growing list and declared that humans were not made in the image of God, but God was made in the image of humans.

Welcome to the *Scientific Revolution*.

Science Nullifies Faith

Between 1600 and 1900, there was a radical shift from theology to science. The world was now being understood on its own, without reference to God or the Bible. For many, there was no longer a need for God because science was now explaining all the mysteries of life. The world was no longer "God's creation" that we are to enjoy; it had become a puzzle for humans to solve.

The conversation regarding science versus faith grew beyond a healthy debate. Faith was getting the boot.

E. O. Wilson was an influential biologist who was nicknamed "The New Darwin." As an atheist, he had no tolerance for the Christian story, stating, "For the sake of human progress, the best thing we could possibly do would be to diminish, to the point of eliminating, religious faiths."[2]

This makes no sense to me.

In this period of the church (1600–1900), some followers of Jesus packed their belongings in a coffin when they traveled to serve in impoverished parts of the world, fully expecting to surrender their lives as part of their passionate efforts to make a difference. They built thousands of schools all over the planet to educate children in both theology and the sciences. They built thousands of hospitals to care for people whom the wealthy and the governments wanted nothing to do with.

These hospitals and schools were not funded by the "Karl Marx Foundation" or the "Charles Darwin Philanthropic Society." They were funded and built by people who believed they were living in a story where Jesus is King. That's why Oxford, Cambridge, Harvard, Yale, Princeton, McGill, and other universities started as theological schools. That's why hospitals have names such as Saint Luke's, Saint John's, and Saint Paul's.

How is it possible to look at the admittedly imperfect church story and conclude that the world would be a better place without followers of Jesus?

It doesn't make sense.

There must be a better relationship between science and faith than win/lose.

Science Focuses Faith

What if science was never supposed to be in competition with faith? What if the Scientific Revolution helped *clarify* the role of faith?

There was a circle of power between the kings and clergy. They supported and protected each other, and the circle was too powerful for any person or group to penetrate. But enlightened citizens were now listening to Twisted Sister: "We're not gonna take it anymore."[3]

We will no longer be oppressed, and we will no longer be silent. This led to a revolution in America, with people seeking "life, liberty, and the pursuit of happiness," and a revolution in France, with people seeking "liberty, equality, and fraternity." They were determined to break the circle of power and create a better world.

Did they? Did the Age of Enlightenment help or hinder the church?

Sometimes Christians freak out when scientists seemingly attempt to nullify faith. "Those scientists can't teach evolution as a scientific fact to our children. They can't verify the age of our earth—it's all just a guess. They can't remove prayer from our schools. They can't decide when a fertilized egg becomes a person."

Followers of Jesus have been deeply concerned about the growing power of science for hundreds of years, but I'm not sure Jesus has been equally troubled. During the eighteenth century, I doubt Jesus ever thought, "Oh no—they've figured it out!"

I'm equally confident that he didn't say to himself, "So *that's* how that works! Dad never explained that one to me."

I imagine him thinking, "Well done. You've figured out the basic formula of how energy is related to mass and the speed of light. You're learning about relativity. Great work. But you are barely scratching the surface. You ain't seen nothing yet!"

Perhaps it's inappropriate to imagine Jesus using poor grammar, but you get the idea.

Science doesn't erode the credibility of faith; it provides focus to faith. The Bible was never intended to be a scientific book explaining the origin of humanity, nor a political treatise on how to organize civilization. It's a true story about three characters: a God who created everything the scientists marvel at, humans who are gifted with the magnificent world around us and the ability to explore it, and an enemy who is effectively using science to create doubt in the minds of God's beloved. The Bible is a story, and the story will always trump science and even theology. It's the blind man who says, "I can't explain it. I simply know that I was blind but now I see." Let science continue to do its thing, and let faith do what only it can do: provide us with the Overall story under which everything else falls.

Science is amazing. Most of us walk around with a supercomputer in our pocket that gives us access to over a million terabytes of information. And—it can even make phone calls. But there's so much about God's creation that we don't understand. It's not that we *use* only ten percent of our brain, it's that we only *understand* ten percent of how it works.[4] We've only explored about five percent of the oceans. We don't know why cats purr, why cows face either north or south, or how an octopus can change color and texture to blend into its surroundings.

Let science continue to do what it can do. And let faith focus on understanding and living in the grand story of God.

Science Fuels Faith

Even better than providing focus to faith, what if science is an injection of fuel to help faith burn hot?

In the seventeenth century, it wasn't science *versus* faith. Science was an exciting exploration and appreciation of all God created. It was the continuation of thoughts from an ancient Hebrew song:

> *Great are the works of the Lord;*
> *they are pondered by all who delight in them.* —*Psalm 111:2*

The deeper we ponder, the greater our delight.

When I was in high school, I listened to Paul Simon, Glass Tiger, and Ratt—among other bands. It's fair to say I didn't have a well-developed appreciation for classical music. In college I joined a fancy *chorale*, which is a just an uppity word for choir. I was learning to sing and play guitar, and I wanted to absorb as much music as I could. Our big project for the season was Mozart's Requiem. We did the whole piece with a professional chorale, Italian soloists, and the Edmonton Symphony Orchestra. I can feel my posture straighten even as I recall the final concert at the Jubilee Auditorium.

Do I now listen to classical music?

No, I still listen to Paul Simon, Glass Tiger, and Ratt. But I do appreciate the Requiem because I know it. I can still sing along to parts of it. The more we understand something, the more we appreciate it. The more we understand a certain sport, the more we appreciate what professional athletes are capable of in that sport. The more we understand someone's history, upbringing, and backstory, the more we can appreciate that person.

The deeper we ponder, the greater our delight.

Bill Bryson's book *The Body: A Guide for Occupants* was a worshipful experience for me. Bryson is an atheist who is annoyed by Christians who want to push their understanding of the story on others, but he composed a book of science that wonderfully fuels my faith. In the first chapter he wrote:

> Altogether it takes 7 billion billion billion atoms to make you. No one can say why those 7 billion billion billion have such an urgent desire to be you. They are mindless particles, after all, without a single thought or notion between them. Yet somehow for the length of your existence, they will build and maintain all the countless systems and structures necessary to keep you humming, to make you you, to give you form and shape and let you enjoy the rare and supremely agreeable condition known as life.[5]

In the margin of my copy I wrote, "This sounds like a psalm!" This sounds like someone who is in awe of our existence. Bryson clarifies that atoms are building blocks, but they are not alive. The basic unit of life is the cell, but it is made up of little items that are not themselves alive. He concludes, "Yet somehow when all of these things are brought together, you have life. That is the part that eludes science."[6]

Somehow indeed.

Science is not challenging the idea of creation—it's appreciating it. It's unlocking evidence as to how beautiful and intricate God's design is. One of the *actual* psalms says it this way:

> *Take notice, you senseless ones among the people;*
> *you fools, when will you become wise?*
> *Does he who fashioned the ear not hear?*
> *Does he who formed the eye not see?* —*Psalm 94:8–9*

Take notice! Don't miss out on the incredible marvels of creation you experience every day. It was God who fashioned the ear. Sound hits the eardrum and creates a vibration that passes into the inner ear, which has over 15,000 hair cells that respond to different frequencies and send messages to the brain. All of this happens instantaneously while we take in all the sounds and tones of Mozart's Requiem. The more we understand the ear, the more we appreciate the one who made it.

It was God who formed the eye, the second most complex organ next to the brain. Light enters the eye through the pupil. It's focused within the eye, then projected onto the retina, which is like a movie screen. That image is upside down, but the brain flips it around for us. We have two eyes for the purpose of depth perception. The brain analyzes the differences between the complex images from each eye and determines how far away something is. The brain receives all this information through a million nerve fibers, which is why we can't do a whole-eye transplant. We can replicate the eye, but we can't reconnect the million nerve fibers.

Thanks to the Scientific Revolution, we know a great deal more about the One who created us. The deeper we ponder, the greater our delight.

---

1. Martin Luther, *Luther's Works, Vol. 54: Table Talk*, ed. Helmut T. Lehmann (Philadelphia: Fortress Press, 1967), 358–359.
2. E. O. Wilson, as quoted at https://www.salon.com/2015/01/28/e_o_wilson_we_should_diminish_to_the_point_of_eliminating_religious_faiths/, accessed May 26, 2022.
3. Twisted Sister was not the most musically mature band in the 1980s, but their tunes were rather catchy.
4. See https://www.scientificamerican.com/article/do-people-only-use-10-percent-of-their-brains/.
5. Bill Bryson, *The Body: A Guide for Occupants* (New York: Doubleday, 2019), 5.
6. Ibid., 6.

5.5 Consumerism (AD 1900–Today)

It was daylight when I entered Notre Dame, the medieval cathedral in Paris. It took a moment for my eyes to adjust to the limited natural lighting inside. The scene before me was breathtaking. I didn't want to take a photo because I knew it could never capture the enormity of the main hall. The reason for tall ceilings in churches was to force people to look up. It was an architectural message that God is big, and this place is where you can encounter him. The message remains very effective.

I was twenty-five years old, and I had the opportunity to wander around Paris by myself for a week. I stepped into numerous other small cathedrals throughout the city that don't have a famous story about a hunchback, and they were all magnificent. The ceilings were tall, the stained-glass windows were gorgeous, and the wood and stone designs were opulent.

It was an unforgettable experience, but it does make you wonder—is that what Jesus had in mind when he said, "Upon this rock I will build my *ekklésia*"?

It's an important question.

Many modern churches have elaborate designs for children's ministry, activity areas for students, and lights and smoke machines in the main auditorium. Is this what Jesus had in mind?

After Jesus' death and resurrection, he coached Peter as the first leader of the church. Three times Jesus asked Peter,

> *"Do you love me?" —John 21:15*

All three times, Peter responded, "Yes." And all three times, Jesus told Peter to care for his sheep.

The leader of a church is a shepherd who is caring for the *lambs* who gather to learn more about the grand story and their role in it. After two thousand years, we have many different types of churches and many approaches to lamb-feeding. We should be amazing at it by now.

Are we? What is the status of the church? Is this what Jesus had in mind when he said to take care of his flock?

Living in Darkness

Matthew's version of the story of Jesus quotes the Old Testament prophet Isaiah:

> *"The people living in darkness*
> *have seen a great light;*
> *on those living in the land of the shadow of death*
> *a light has dawned."* —*Matthew 4:16*

Isaiah was talking about the city of Jerusalem. The Israelites thought their capital city, God's city, could never fall. How could darkness come to the city that is supposed to reflect the glory of the Lord?

Matthew was talking about Jesus, who would soon reveal himself to the people living in darkness.

The church has certainly seen her share of darkness in the form of persecution, crusades, inquisitions, arrogance, and martyrdom.

Unfortunately, the darkness continued in the twentieth century. It started with the Great War that took the lives of over 20 million people. The Depression of the 1930s led to a desperate Germany that put its hope in the Nazi Party. Over 85 million people died in the Second World War, including the horrific loss of six million Jews.

The 1970s were anti-everything. Anti-war, anti-government, anti-religion, anti-good-taste-in-music. Traditional churches were steadily losing relevance.

The 1980s were awesome and the world experienced very little moral decline during that time.

That last sentence is, of course, not true. I was a child of the 80s and like to pretend that all was well. Nonetheless, the 1900s were a century of waning interest in the church and the overall message of Jesus. They saw the secularization of the western world, meaning that Christian values were steadily being replaced by humanistic ones. More and more people were walking away from the light and living in darkness.

A Bold New Idea

So the church came up with a bold new idea: what if church was fun? What if church was no longer a painful Sunday morning experience, sitting on a piece of wood for two hours, trying to keep your eyes open like you were driving at night on the highway?

The first idea was to provide a better learning environment for children during Sunday morning services. This made sense because few five-year-olds, for example, are naturally interested in "the substitutionary atonement of the crucifixion."

The idea expanded to teenagers so they could have their own space to share, process, and sit upside-down on Goodwill couches.

The game-changer in the 1980s was when church leaders started designing Sunday mornings for *visitors* rather than regular attendees. Unchurched people were polled to determine why they were not attending. As a result, seats became softer, messages became shorter, and topics were driven more by what people wanted to hear than what people might need to hear. I remember being a young worship leader tasked with the job of inspiring a hymnal-reading church to look up at the portable screen and read the lyrics from an overhead projector. I enjoyed playing guitar in that church, but I didn't appreciate the weekly glares from the resistant regulars.

With theatrics, music, video, lighting, graphics, and cafés, the church was making the experience as comfortable, inviting, and non-threatening as possible. I get that. I'm fully on board with that. I've spent the last twenty-five years of my life making decisions aligned with that.

But the question remains: Is this what Jesus meant by "Upon this rock I will build my *ekklésia*" and "Feed my lambs"?

Even huge churches that have been wonderfully successful by offering "fun" church experiences are asking themselves if their people are getting fed.

What is the status of the church now? What is the condition of the millions of new believers who have been reached during this bold new idea?

Unintended Result

The church growth movement has been a valiant effort. It was born out of a passion for people who are far from Jesus. It was modeled after Jesus himself, who was a courageous friend of sinners.

But it has created an unintended result: consumers.

People who come to church to be entertained usually stay at church to be entertained. People who choose a church based on the singing voice of the worship leader or the personality of the speaker usually leave for the same reason. Churches that used to be filled with disciples are now populated with consumers. Targeting the unchurched has been very successful, but while there has been significant growth in numbers, there has been questionable growth in depth.

The church I pastored in Phoenix, Arizona, offered an inexpensive weekend mission trip to build simple homes in Rocky Point, Mexico. We had more demanding trips to other parts of the world, but this was a terrific introduction for our previously unchurched people.

A young couple paid the $65 fee for the two-day experience. They were furious when they arrived in Mexico and discovered the rooms had no air conditioning and the mattresses were not Posturepedic. They went to a nearby resort and paid $385 for the two nights' stay. When they returned to Phoenix, they complained about the experience to anyone who would listen, and demanded the church reimburse them for the $385.

I'm not sure they fully understood the concept of a mission trip.

Somehow, somewhere, there has been a shift in why people gather as followers of Jesus. If we are to continue the revolution of love, then we must remember that we're here to *serve* the mission of the church, not be served by it. In the oft-mentioned comparison between dogs and cats, dogs are excited when you come home, while cats are thankful the staff has arrived. What I'm saying is—don't be a cat. Don't prowl around the church expecting to be served. Look for opportunities to serve in a meaningful way. Don't be a consumer. Don't choose a church because it has the funniest speaker or the coolest worship leader.

Choose a church for the *ekklésia*—the community of imperfect people who will likely be there long after your favorite pastor has moved on.

I'm thrilled the Rocky Point couple attended our church, and I fully believe that any nudge in the right direction is an expansion of God's kingdom. But what can be done to address consumerism in the church? What has her two-thousand-year story taught us?

Appealing and Challenging

The twentieth century showed us that the church can and should be *appealing*. It's irresponsible to lead a ministry and just expect people to be interested in whatever is said and done. Leaders need to be creative. And provocative. They need to imagine themselves as participants and consider what would help someone pay attention, remember, and want to participate.

For example, C. S. Lewis was a brilliant light in the middle of the darkening twentieth century. He was beautifully appealing in his writings about the grand story. He didn't just write about the tactics of the evil third character in the story; he wrote about the exchange between a senior demon and his nephew, a junior tempter (*The Screwtape Letters*). He didn't just write about the theology of heaven and hell; he wrote about a group of people from hell taking a bus trip to heaven (*The Great Divorce*). He didn't just write about the mighty power of Jesus; he wrote about four children entering a wardrobe and being transported to Narnia to meet Aslan the lion (*The Chronicles of Narnia*).

We don't have to have the creative genius of C. S. Lewis. But telling the grand story in a creative way is worthy of our best efforts. A math teacher can write out the perfectly correct answers on the board, but the good ones try to make it interesting for the kids who don't like math.

The church has a responsibility to bring creativity to the message. Opposing the church growth movement for being entertainment-focused is not an excuse for being boring and lifeless.

Jesus wasn't. He was incredibly appealing. He told humorous and relevant stories and gathered crowds who strained to hear every word he had to say. Generosity is more appealing than an impressive facility. Authenticity is more appealing than perceived perfection. The church can and should be appealing.

The two-thousand-year church story also teaches us that she must be *challenging*. We explored this in Chapter 3.4 through the words of Jesus:

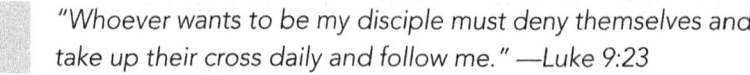

> *"Whoever wants to be my disciple must deny themselves and take up their cross daily and follow me."* —*Luke 9:23*

The church is not supposed to use people for her gain (Crusades) or take something from people (indulgences). She's supposed to feed people who are hungry for physical or spiritual food.

God's design is for us to be in *ekklésia* together—not just hear the grand story and move on but be regularly challenged by it for the rest of our lives. Whether you currently attend a church or you're looking for one, what is your expectation each week? Do you want to be entertained or challenged? Are you ready to put every part of your life on the table and say, "God, have your way—which part of my life do you want to challenge this week?"

In general, church is not supposed to be a big show. It's supposed to be a big deal.

At the church I pastored in Phoenix, we had a phrase written across a fifty-foot wall in the lobby: "A safe place to visit…a dangerous place to stay."

I once heard my young daughter misquote the phrase to a friend. She said, "Our church is a safe place to visit…and a horrible place to stay."

So close.

Some in the church had the opinion that my daughter's version was more accurate, but that's always the plight of a pastor.

My daughter was not alone in her confusion. Some guests would read the sign and tilt their heads like a dog trying to understand strange words. We're a safe place (appealing); we want people to feel welcomed, loved, and not judged. And we're a dangerous place (challenging); we want people to think differently about God, themselves, and others. In other words, come as you are—but please don't stay that way!

Let me be clear, we didn't have it all figured out. We were great at the "safe" part but constantly struggled with what it meant to be "dangerous." The words were a declaration of our intent more than a description of our reality.

The best way to balance *appeal* and *challenge* in the church is to continuously direct people to Jesus. In Acts 2, the church started with the miraculous power of the Holy Spirit. Then humans took over and attained significant power in the church down through the fifteenth century. The Reformation challenged the role of the clergy, and the Scientific Revolution offered a secular replacement for that power. Near the end of the twentieth century, the bold new idea was to hand power to the seekers in the community. Let *them* decide what the church does and how she does it.

When perusing the whole story of the church, it seems things went best when the Holy Spirit was in charge.

A Great Light

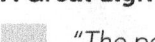

> *"The people living in darkness have seen a great light."*
> *—Matthew 4:16 (quoting Isaiah 9:2)*

The role of the church is to reclaim what darkness has stolen. Have you ever woken up with high hopes for a great day—your body feels great, the birds are singing, the coffee maker is working beautifully? Then you get a phone call, see a text, read an e-mail, join a meeting—and darkness comes. Darkness is not passive. It's not bad luck and it's not something that happens accidently. It's an attack.

During the terrorist plane hijackings of September 11, 2001, darkness made a brutal attack on hope in the United States. It backfired, though, because people flocked to churches and responded with tremendous courage and strength. Darkness continues to plot. What would it take to keep people away from church—possibly even shut churches down? What could possibly happen that would cause followers of Jesus to divide, live in fear, and fight among themselves?

A virus.

COVID-19 was terrifically effective, beginning in 2020. The disease forced churches to reevaluate strategies and practices. And it led many regular attendees to stay at home on Sunday mornings.

Darkness is not passive. But the 2,700-year-old promise remains—people living in darkness will see a great light.

Jesus never gave up on the world when we were hellbent on killing one another through the two World Wars. He never gave up on a generation that wanted to smoke pot and enjoy "free love." He never gave up on western countries sinking deeper into secularization. He never gave up on you when you were sowing your wild oats and ignored him for years. He never gave up on you when you thought you were better than others.

Jesus, the Great Light, never gave up. And he won't stop now.

Jesus set the church up to be empowered by the Holy Spirit. He wants his church to be irresistibly appealing and courageously challenging. He never gave up on the grand story—and he won't stop now.

PART VI:
LIFE

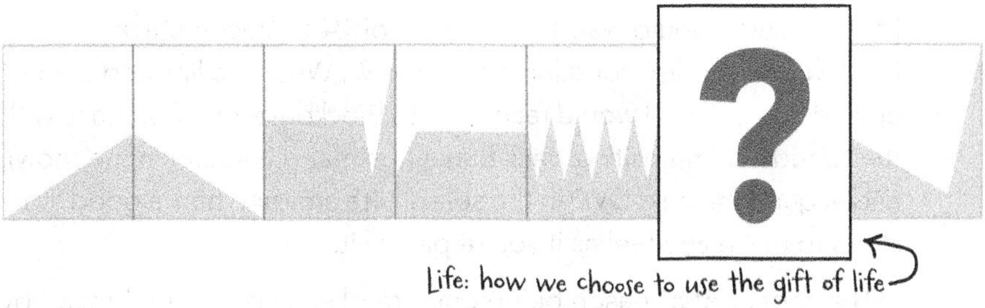
?
Life: how we choose to use the gift of life

Intro

This section is different. There's a question mark on the *why-axis* graph above because there's no predetermined framework for this part of the story. The two-by-fours for this section are unique to you, and many of them will be created *by* you. This section is the extraordinary reality that you are *part* of the Overall story. The Bible is not just a series of ancient writings we are to read, study, and reflect on. It's an invitation *into* the story. We have a significant role to play—as do our children and our children's children. Our decisions, successes, failures, struggles, and weaknesses matter a great deal. You are not just performing a task, raising a family, or doing the best job you can. You are a history-maker. You are part of the story.

When I was young, television was different. Each episode of a show was a stand-alone story. The bad guy was introduced at the beginning of every episode (he was typically a male and often the same actor who played the bad guy on other shows). Then the Duke boys, or the

A-Team, or Crockett and Tubbs would interact with said bad guy, who would end up in handcuffs at the end of the show, mumbling something such as, "I almost got away with it...." The show would end with a catchy theme song, and we would look forward to next week. There was no continuing story, no grand narrative, and no need to watch the shows in order.

In 2001, the world was introduced to a new television show simply called *24*. It did not have seasons with isolated episodes. Each season captured the events of a single day, told in twenty-four episodes. One episode covered one hour of that day and flowed directly into the next. Those who are familiar with this show can hear the pounding beats of every second as you continue in and out of commercials. My wife and I would wait for a season of *24* to become available on DVD, with each disc containing four shows. When we finished the last episode on a DVD, I would race back to Blockbuster Video, run in with the speed and intensity of Jack Bauer (the main character in the show), and acquire the next DVD in the season. It's amazing how a good story starts to make you feel as if you're part of it.

This format of a season being one grand story is now embraced by nearly every television show. We don't want isolated pieces. We want the big picture. We don't want a pile of lumber; we want a framework we can build on.

The Marvel Cinematic Universe (MCU) took this concept into the area of film. What if a movie was more than just an isolated story? What if there was a grand narrative beyond a movie and its sequel, or even a trilogy of movies?

The MCU began with the movie *Iron Man*. They didn't have an overall plan at first; they just wanted to make a great movie. But the director, Jon Favreau, gifted the viewers with a hint of a grand idea. It was a bonus scene after all the credits rolled that was not shown during any of the pre-screening or for the critics. It was saved for opening weekend. They revealed a secret that Samuel L. Jackson would be cast as Nick Fury. His character saunters out of the darkness into a hint of light and says to the lead character of *Iron Man*, "Mr. Stark, you've become part of a bigger universe. You just don't know it yet."

The fans on opening weekend went crazy. They loved it. They wanted more.

You are designed to be part of a grand story. Your life is not an irrelevant, isolated narrative. You are a part of a bigger universe. You just may not know it yet.

In this section, we'll explore the story of your life. You are not one episode of a television show. You are way more complicated than that. The two-by-fours of your life assemble a narrative that is embedded into the Overall story. Imagine looking at your life as a scriptwriter would lay out the plan for a season of a TV series. You're currently in episode six (or twelve, or eighteen) and all the episodes somehow fit together.

6.1 Final Episode

Ever climbed into an Uber and said, "I don't care where you go—just go somewhere"? It's unlikely because the driver won't come pick you up until you have entered a destination. Ever gone to an airport with a passport and a packed bag and said to the person behind the counter, "Surprise me"? Once again, unlikely. We typically have a destination, a plan, a place we're intending to go.

What about life in general? Do you have a destination or a plan? Or are you wandering from day to day, relationship to relationship, job to job, hobby to hobby? At times we're heading toward something beautiful—an island with palm trees and fresh water—only to discover that it's just a mirage. It's fake. Then we're confused, and we really don't know which direction to head next.

As of this writing, the Marvel Cinematic Universe continues to make movies, but the central narrative ran for twenty-two films, from *Iron Man* in 2008 to *Endgame* in 2019. During that time, they gradually introduced the concept of *infinity stones*, which were essential to the final movie, and they introduced the anti-hero, *Thanos*, in a post-credit scene in *The Avengers* in 2012. Throughout the process, they didn't have all the details laid out, but they had a general idea of where they were going. They knew what their *Endgame* was.

In the story of our lives, we are wise to identify the end game. What do you hope to accomplish with the rest of your days? What do you want your final episode to look like? Consider the second of seven habits recommended by author and successful businessman Stephen Covey: Begin with the end in mind.[1] If you don't know what the target is, you won't know where to aim.

Get the Prize

All three of our kids ran cross-country. It was new to me because when I was in school, running was not a sport—it was punishment. These kids ran their hearts out. All of them. I never understood why parents would stand on the course and yell, "Run faster!"

Do these parents expect their kids to say, "*That's* what I was supposed to be doing! I totally forgot. Thanks, observant parent!"?

The way I see it, cross-country running is how the motivated, disciplined kids experience the "party" side of high school: with rock music blaring over the speakers, runners would come flopping into the finish area, vomit as needed, and say "I love you, man" to the volunteers giving them something to drink. So similar.

In high school competition, they run 3.1 miles. The race wouldn't work if it was an unknown distance—if they were told to run hard until they heard a siren, then stop. They need a finish line. They need a target.

Corinth was a Greek city and very familiar with the Olympic Games of ancient Greece. The most popular sport was running, which is why Paul wrote to the people of Corinth,

> *Do you not know that in a race all the runners run, but only one gets the prize? Run in such a way as to get the prize.*
> *—1 Corinthians 9:24*

When I ran my one marathon, I didn't have hopes of winning the race. I think the winner was interviewed, showered, and finished with lunch by the time I crossed the finish line. This had absolutely no effect on the joy I experienced when I received my medal, the prize that says I finished the race.

In the race Paul was writing about, all of us can win the prize if we keep running. I won't walk, and I won't lie down on the side of the road. I'll keep running to the best of my ability, and I'll inspire others to run their best as well, because their victory takes nothing away from mine.

At the end of your life, what would it look like for you to get the prize?

Years ago, I did an exercise where I wrote my own eulogy. What would I want to be said about me at the end of my life? At first I wrote, *He was so witty, intimidatingly handsome, and relentlessly humble.*

But the exercise quickly became very meaningful. I was in college at the time, and it forced me to think about my deeply rooted ambitions. Why am I considering this career? At the end of my days, what will true success look like? It helps clarify the value of relationships and the foolishness of worldly pursuits. What do you want people to say about you? That you were impressively fit? That you amassed great wealth? That your home was consistently neat and tidy?

What does it mean for you to *get the prize*? If you don't paint that picture for yourself, the world will paint it for you.

Strict Training

In the next verse, Paul clarified how we can win that prize:

> *Everyone who competes in the games goes into strict training.*
> *—1 Corinthians 9:25*

I've heard people say, "Wow, you're so lucky. You're so fast. It must be nice to run a mile in less than six minutes."

I've never heard people say that to *me*, of course. But I've heard people say that to *other* runners. Anyone who says those words fails to understand the amount of work it takes to run that fast. Sub-six-minute runners are not lucky. They wake up early in the morning and commit to strict training.

Many of us have been told that we have "great potential" by a parent, a coach, or a teacher. Those are inspiring words, but great potential is not enough to win the prize. Identifying natural abilities and enjoying early success is not the same as enjoying the fullness of God's plan for you. That takes consistent and disciplined attention. Winning the prize is not something that happens *to* you. It's an active experience. It's something we train for one week at a time, one decision at a time, one relationship at a time. It's easy to *have* potential; it's hard to fulfill it.

Every episode of your life is moving toward the final episode. Either we are developing something that helps make the end game extraordinary, or we are wasting opportunities that can never be recovered.

My Final Episode

Let me give you an example from my own journey and what I desire for my final episode. While I was writing this chapter, my wife sent me a text with the following verses from the Old Testament:

> *I'm thanking you, GOD, from a full heart,*
> *I'm writing the book on your wonders.*
> *I'm whistling, laughing, and jumping for joy;*
> *I'm singing your song, High God.*
> *—Psalm 9:1–2 (The Message)*

I want to enjoy every episode of life. I want to be content in all situations, as Paul modeled. I don't want fame, power, or money because I don't trust myself with any of them. I want a legacy of joy. The *why-axis* graph for Part VI (Life) is a question mark because we get to decide what success looks like, and our decisions determine whether we get the prize. For me, I choose joy.

It's how I read the Bible: I love seeing real people and humor in the stories. It's how I connect with people: I love it when my wife laughs so hard she tears up and her face turns red. I thrive at work when I'm on a team of people who are as joyful as they are passionate. My best friends in life are the people I laugh hysterically with. For me, laughter is not a smokescreen for the deep stuff—it's the pathway.

I see people in their final episode of life who have lost their joy. Gravity has pulled their skin down, and despair has pulled joy down with it. I'm not evaluating them; I'm simply saying that I don't want that for me. I have always had an obnoxious laugh. It's a very explosive sound that is not suitable for indoors. I dream of the eighty-seven-year-old, final-episode version of me still experiencing the occasional explosion of laughter. I want a legacy of joy. That's my prize.

It won't just happen to me, so here's how I plan to get there.

First, I *value* people in my life who bring me joy. The older I get, the rarer they seem to be. I choose to invest time and money into those precious relationships. These are the people I explore the deepest levels with. These are the people who have earned the right to challenge me on anything and redirect me when I take my eyes off Jesus and the Overall story.

Second, I fiercely *attack* any resentment cells in my body. When I walk around with resentment toward those whom I believe have hurt me, it kills my joy. Unfortunately, my natural desire for control leads me to protect those self-destructive cells. My final-episode joy requires me to forgive others and recognize how often I have been the offender.

Third, I *capture* memories. I have three journals: one for work, one for family, and one that is personal. I don't fill them with bitterness because I want to let go of the nasty stuff. I fill them with learnings I want to remember and joy I want to revisit. I organize and label all our photos, and I have edited a one-hour family video for each year since our first child was born. If my brain starts to have gaps in recalling the joys of life, I want my "strict training" to help fill them in.

That's *my* why-axis. It's what I hope for *my* final episode. It's not the only answer. So—what about you?

Your Final Episode

How do you want the story of your life to end? What do you want people to say about you as they celebrate your life? If you've ever had the pleasure of spending time with people in their final episode, it's unlikely you heard them celebrate how much money they made, or how many hours they worked, or which risks they avoided.

Whatever episode you're currently in, it's wise to pause and paint a picture in your mind of how you want your story to end. My suggestion is to be mindful of the two extremes.

Imagine a final episode that is *attainable*. Don't paint a picture that is out of your control or beyond your reach. Some say their goal in life is to see the grandkids graduate and attend their weddings. That's beautiful, but it's outside of your control. You get to shape your relationships with them, but you don't get to make decisions for them.

Your final episode should not be dependent on others. It should be something God wants to do in and through you.

In my example, joy is under my control. Regardless of the circumstances, I can always choose joy.

Considering the other extreme, imagine a final episode that is *audacious*. Don't paint a picture that's too simple or perhaps even already accomplished. You have episodes remaining in your life, and they should matter. Can you imagine a final episode that is grander than your financial security? deeper than people saying how nice you were? more demanding than people saying how much you enjoyed golf? Can you imagine a final episode where people in your community or your city, or even people around the world, would say about you, "My life has been transformed by the power of Jesus because of that person"?

In my example, joy is elusive, and it naturally fades. I want my family to continue to see the joy of the Lord in me. I want anyone who is interested to know that I'm excited to experience the next stage of my relationship with Jesus.

Only So Many Days

The band Switchfoot has a song that asks the question, "This is your life, are you who you want to be?"

It's a beautifully piercing question. You get one shot at it—one set of days. We can repair mistakes, but we can't go back in time. Are you willing to pause in the busyness of life and reflect on whether you've clearly defined what success looks like? Are you willing to be honest about whether you're heading in the right direction?

Every day is a gift from God, and your life has only so many of them.

> *This is the day the Lord has made;*
> *We will rejoice and be glad in it.*
> *—Psalm 118:24 (New King James Version)*

How many days are we willing to waste? Unfortunately, I've had plenty of them. While brushing my teeth at night I have wondered, "What happened to this day?" I've had days where I was not ill but couldn't get out of bed. I've had days where I have wallowed in my anger. I've had days where I have watched Marvel movies from sunup to sundown (although I might argue that those were rather terrific days for me and my family).

This is your life, are you who you want to be?

1. Stephen R. Covey, *The 7 Habits of Highly Effective People* (New York: Simon & Schuster, 1989).

6.2 Previous Episodes

Have you ever exploded with anger at a customer, someone in your home, or the driver in another vehicle and thought, "Where did *that* come from?" You were fine immediately before the moment. There was nothing brewing or stewing inside you that you were aware of. Then *wham!* Have you ever felt compelled to do something to yourself that you know is not healthy either physically or emotionally—and you're puzzled because it seems others don't share the same compulsion? Have you ever suddenly shut down beyond your control? There's some button that gets pushed by someone else's actions or words, and you lock down like a clam. You wish you could simply get over it, but you can't—at least not for a while.

There's always a story behind that stuff.

If your life is like one season of a television show, then today is not episode one. There have been previous episodes that must be understood before you can make sense of your current episode. Sometimes it's important to watch the "Previously on..." introduction.

You've seen this clearly in other people's stories. The guy who is dreadfully impatient with the server at a restaurant or hotel. The mom who blames every teacher for her child's behavior. There's always a story. The jogger in your neighborhood who won't wave back no matter how friendly you try to be. The gossiper at work who gets more excited as the information gets more damaging. There's a story behind every apparent jerk.

Unplowed Ground

This chapter is about unearthing our previous episodes. We tend to bury the painful and embarrassing parts of our story with the hope that others won't know and we can forget. But we can't experience the final episode we desire until we are honest about our past and liberated from it.

Jeremiah was one of the prophets before the exile. He was speaking to a stubborn group of people who were not acknowledging their disobedience. He told them,

> *"Break up your unplowed ground."* —*Jeremiah 4:3*

You must go into your previous episodes and swing a pickaxe. The further back you go and the deeper the wound, the more packed the ground will be. This is the *path* Jesus spoke about where the seed can't penetrate the hard surface. Nothing grows in unplowed ground. No peaches, no apples, no strawberries. No delicious fruit of any kind. When previous episodes are ignored or sugarcoated, the hurt, pain, and destruction continue to show up.

This is not about salvation. We are free to learn the grand story, accept Jesus as Lord, yet retain unplowed ground. For comparison, I can remain married to my wife and refuse to talk with her about mistakes I've made. This wouldn't mean I don't have a relationship with her, but it would mean that we are unlikely to have a great marriage story. Retaining unplowed ground in life will have a negative effect on all relationships (including our relationship with God) and all future episodes.

This is the difference between healed Christians and plastic Christians. Healed Christians have soft soil. There is significant growth, but it took a lot of work and it was messy. Plastic Christians set tables up on the packed soil and wrap them in tablecloths. They host lovely parties, talk about how wonderful life is, and hide their pain and loneliness. Plastic Christians are unwilling to say more than "Fine," "Super," "Great," or "Terrific" whenever someone cares enough to ask how they're doing. It's not believable and it's not attractive.

Start With the *Why*

For some, breaking up unplowed ground is a ridiculous idea. Why stir up pain from the past? If it's buried under packed soil, why not leave it there? What happened in the past should stay in the past.

That plan sounds reasonable—but it's not. The past doesn't stay in the past. It leaks out through our thoughts, words, and actions.

In Chapter 3.2, I mentioned Jesus' longest recorded speech, known as the Sermon on the Mount. It's a wonderfully practical challenge for those who choose to follow Jesus. He concluded his famous speech with these words:

> *"Therefore everyone who hears these words of mine and puts them into practice is like a wise man who built his house on the rock. The rain came down, the streams rose, and the winds blew and beat against that house; yet it did not fall, because it had its foundation on the rock. But everyone who hears these words of mine and does not put them into practice is like a foolish man who built his house on sand." —Matthew 7:24–26*

So many lives are built on previous episodes of deception, coverup, embarrassment, guilt, and shame. The reason we respond in ways that are selfish, prideful, and hurtful is that our house is built on sand. It could crumble at any moment, and we know it.

When we're honest about our past—about the awful things that have happened to us as well as the poor decisions we've made—then our house gets built on the rock. It may be a smaller house for now. Some people get courageously honest and end up losing a job, a marriage, or the respect of others. It's painful, but the truth will set you free. It's better to have a shack built on the rock than a mansion built on the sand.

Over a period of years, my wife and I watched some friends advance from a tiny little home to an enormous place in our community. It's the American dream. They started from one modest income and very little space for their two children to play. Then she got a full-time job. He got a huge promotion that involved significant travel. And he spent a lot of time with his secretary. Too much time. Our friends bought a huge house so they could enjoy the fruit of their labor. As a result, the kids had so much space that mom and dad barely saw them. After this couple divorced, the wife told us, "Life was so much better in that little house. It was small and chaotic, but it was honest, and we were much happier."

I'm not challenging the desire to get a bigger home. I'm sharing this as a metaphor for our spiritual and emotional health. It's better to have a modest, overcrowded house built on the rock than an impressive and spacious palace built on the sand.

This is what happens when people hit *rock bottom*. Life has crumbled over the shifting sand, and stability doesn't happen until all the sand is gone and all that's left is the rock. Some people need to hit rock bottom before they are willing to look honestly at their previous episodes. Rock bottom is effective, but it's not necessary. God provided warning after warning to the Israelites before the exile, and he continues to provide us with reminders along the way. All we need to do is speak the truth *now*—and our lives can be reconstructed on the rock.

That's what happened with a wee little man named Zacchaeus. He was a wealthy but miserable tax collector (same profession as Matthew from Chapter 3.1). He climbed a tree so he could see Jesus, the one he believed could provide him with a better story. Jesus saw him, called him down, and insisted on visiting him at his home. Could you imagine? Zacchaeus was hoping to catch a glimpse of the famous rabbi and he ended up having dinner with him.

Zacchaeus desperately wanted freedom from his old episodes and declared,

> *"Look, Lord! Here and now I give half of my possessions to the poor, and if I have cheated anybody out of anything, I will pay back four times the amount." —Luke 19:8*

Jesus didn't ask him to do anything. He didn't ask Zacchaeus to pay back anyone. Why was he so eager? Why was he so willing to aggressively explore the mistakes from his past and surrender his wealth?

Because he wanted a different story.

He didn't like who he had become. He didn't like how he felt about himself when he woke up in the morning. He didn't like how he was treating people and how they were responding to him. He was tired of being resentful toward people he was supposed to love. Zacchaeus was willing to have less and possibly live in a smaller "home"—as long as that home was built on the rock.

Why should we break up unplowed ground? Because it's a pathway to living a different and better story.

Delta Moments

If you're willing to explore significant moments from the previous chapters of your life, I invite you to participate in an assignment. I haven't asked much of you yet, so please don't complain about the workload!

If you've done this already through counseling or a recovery program, terrific. Review your story and see if there's anything that needs to be added.

Get a piece of paper or take a page in a notebook and write at the top *Delta Moments.* In math and science, *delta* means change. The symbol for delta is a little triangle (Greek letter) one puts in front of a variable such as "x" or in front of a changing value such as "T" for temperature. We're going to make a list of delta moments in your life where something significant changed in your mind, your heart, or your soul. A delta moment changes how you view God, life, eternity, marriage, family, yourself, etc.

Draw a line down the center of the page. On the left side, make a list of such moments. These could be painful events that were caused *by* you—mistakes you made, things you wish you could undo. Or they could be traumatic experiences that happened *to* you—things that were no fault of your own but caused something inside you to change. It could be a move to a new city or school. A word or phrase someone said to you. A dramatic change in a significant relationship. A lucky break. A painful failure. Walk slowly through elementary school…middle school…high school…college…each decade of your adult life.

On the left side of the paper, summarize the delta moments. On the right side, identify what changed. As a result of that moment, how did you think differently about God, others, yourself?

When I was in middle school and heading out the door one day to hang out with my friends, my mom told me she was going to spend some time in a hotel. She never came back, and no one explained to me what happened or why it happened. My dad, my two brothers, and I simply shuffled the chores around and kept moving forward. I learned (right side of the page) that family relationships were unstable, and that when crisis comes, you don't talk about it.

This is one of many delta moments in my story. That event was important because it continues to affect my relationships and my conversations. Your list is not simply a collection of negative events in your life; it's a list of moments (positive or negative) that have shaped who you are.

Control Factors

The second thing I encourage you to do with that list of delta moments is to identify *control factors* throughout your story. In Chapter 3.1, we explored the idea that Jesus came as the solution to our problem of control. In many areas of our lives, we want control, but we can't have it. As you reflect on the "Previously on..." summary of your life, has there been a person, a substance, a pursuit, an interest, or an addiction that has consistently demonstrated control over you?

There may be one control factor that dominates in your story, or there may be a few. Control factors take root early and continue to grow until they are rooted out. As a challenge to one of the new Mediterranean churches, Paul wrote,

> *You were taught, with regard to your former way of life,...*
> *—Ephesians 4:22*

Paul was clear with them about the significance of their previous chapters:

> *...to put off your old self, which is being corrupted by its deceitful desires; to be made new in the attitude of your minds; and to put on the new self. —Ephesians 4:22–24*

He then addressed the role of the third character in the story:

> *Do not give the devil a foothold. —Ephesians 4:27*

Control factors are not generic or universal. The enemy uses delta moments from our lives to identify powerful and unique control factors to sabotage our spiritual growth. One person's debilitating control factor is a non-issue for someone else. All the enemy needs to do is get a foothold—to know what unique temptation is most likely to have control over you.

Based on my previous episodes, my struggle is gaming. Something happens in my brain chemistry when I play poker on my phone. I have irrationally poor stopping mechanisms, and I have experienced the damage of losing control in this area of my life. When things get difficult, I sometimes choose to escape rather than deal with them head on (something I learned in middle school when my mom left). I escape parts of my life I can't control by getting consumed with a game I *can* control—which is ironic because the game has tremendous control over me. During bad seasons, I would regularly spend twenty to thirty minutes in the restroom so I could play a few rounds of poker in private. My sweet mother-in-law assumed I had some serious gastrointestinal issues. Based on my previous episodes, this is not a healthy way for me to "take a break." It's a problem. I have wasted many hours and even resorted to deception in order to hide my foolish interest in online poker. I must be very intentional about fighting the enemy's efforts to keep me distracted.

I once shared my struggle with gaming on a Sunday morning at my church. In the lobby, a long-time attender and leader looked at me with a disgusted face and said, "Gaming?"

I looked at her with an equally disgusted face and said, "Hypocrite?"

No, I didn't. But I wanted to.

Please resist the temptation to evaluate someone else's control factor. If it's something you don't struggle with, it's natural to look down on those who do. Those who have no issue with alcohol can't fathom the profound feeling of helplessness of those who do. People with high metabolism may have little respect for those who wrestle with overeating. Instead of evaluating the control factors of others, we are wise to look at our own story and prepare to counteract what the enemy has planned for us.

I didn't share my struggle with gaming to gain favor with you as the reader. I believe the opposite is more likely. I'm not trying to impress you with my embarrassing admission of weakness; I'm trying to inspire you to identify your own footholds. If your issue is drugs, alcohol, gambling, sex, pornography, or spending money, then you're likely aware of the significance of your past. But there are so many other life-changing distractions out there: social media, video streaming, sports, working out, laziness, sugar, dieting, gossip, vanity, arrogance, insecurity, anger, isolation. And I know I'm not the only person who has experienced the illogical snare of gaming or social media on phones and computers. The power and beauty of technology come with incalculable consequences.

Are you aware of your weak spots? Can you see patterns from your previous episodes that continue to affect you today? It's rarely one thing that we struggle with. It's usually a cocktail of control factors. You're not too old, too macho, too weak, or too broken to do this.

Break up your unplowed ground.

6.3 Current Episode

Now what are we supposed to do?

We have stirred up these deep, significant, and often painful memories from the past. We have unearthed these moments where we have been hurt and where we have hurt others. We have identified *control factors* that have irrational power over us. How does this process help us today during our current episode of life?

Some of the stories from our previous episodes have been dealt with. They don't resurface in destructive ways because we have forgiven others or sought forgiveness. But other stories are still very much alive. They lead us to believe we're broken, untrustworthy, insignificant, ugly, stupid, mean, unlovable, selfish. We believe these lies and accept these limitations.

What would it look like for us to think differently (as we explored in Chapter 4.3) about our previous episodes?

My favorite stage as a dad was when my kids were between nine and eighteen months old. It was ridiculously exhausting but overwhelmingly rewarding. I loved watching them try to stand, then wobble and collapse. I loved holding my arms out as they leaned forward to take their first steps.

When they fell, they didn't get discouraged. I'm not sure they knew that was an option. They looked up at Mom or me, got a huge smile on their face, and stood up to try again. and again. and again.

Tami and I never thought, "Well, I guess he's not a walker."

I don't ever recall saying, "Let's give up on him—we'll try again with the next kid and hope she's good enough." Nope, we knew he could do it. We weren't upset with him when he fell. We smiled and cheered him on.

What if our stumbles in life were not viewed as failures, but simply part of the process of growth? What if our brokenness was viewed from a different perspective?

I would like you to pause and consider one more assignment. That's two assignments in back-to-back chapters. I know it's asking a lot, but I assure you this is the last of the assignments in this book. Would you consider pausing this chapter, looking back on your previous episodes, and rewriting them from God's perspective? Start with your earliest memory and redo your story as if it were God writing it. How would God describe the circumstances of your *delta moments*? How would God describe the control factors you tend to wrestle with? Remember that there are two levels on the stage of life. Our lives play out on the lower level. What do you imagine God was thinking, planning, and doing on the upper level during your previous episodes?

Go ahead, rewrite your story. I'll wait....

No, you didn't even pause! You just jumped to this next sentence! I know because it's what I would do if I was reading this book. But please give it a shot. Your current and future episodes will benefit from you viewing your past differently.

Overlooked

Welcome back.

What did you notice about your story? Were you able to think differently about any key moments? about God? about yourself? My hope is that you were able to see something profoundly consistent through every previous episode of your life:

God.

Loves.

You.

He never wanted to catch you in the act, trap you, or hold you down. He was cheering for you every step of the way. Whenever you stumbled, he didn't write you off. He cheered for you to get up and try again. and again. and again. As you experience your current episode, it's critical that you understand how much God loves you. This is important because sometimes we set those words aside like a meaningless bumper sticker.

"God loves you."

"Great, thanks. Now, let's talk about the important and relevant stuff."

It's like troubleshooting a car engine that won't start. It'll turn over but it won't fire up. You research all sorts of articles and videos on the Internet. You plug the machine into the car computer and interpret its diagnostics. You explore potential issues with the fuel mixture and the oxygen sensors. After hours of futility, you realize—it was out of gas.

When life gets very complicated, frustrating, and hopeless, we are wise to check in on the basics. As you assemble the framework of God's magnificent story, *do not* overlook the reality and beauty of God's love for you.

What Is Love?

So what does it mean to receive love from an omnipotent, quintessential being? It's simpler to bop our heads with The Roxbury Guys[1] than to honestly explore the answer to this question.

When my son Martin was a young teenager, I picked him up from church one night and he said, "Dad, I love you," as we were walking to the car. I asked him if he said that because he wouldn't stop playing basketball and forced me to wait so long.

"No, they told us in church tonight to say that to our parents or siblings."

"That's great, son. I love you too. And I think it would be terrific if you said that to your brother or sister."

That night as the kids were getting ready for bed, he looked up at me, said "Watch this," then went to his sister's closed door and said, "I love you, Lila."

In a very calm but clear voice she replied, "Yechhh." Martin looked up at me and smiled.

We're all a little confused as to what the word *love* really means. Some describe it as a feeling. Others adamantly disagree and declare that it's an action: even when we don't *feel* love toward others, we can *choose* to love them. Perhaps it's both. Perhaps love is given through action and received as a feeling. We show love by washing the dishes, saying a kind word, showing up on time, buying or making a thoughtful gift, shoveling snow from the sidewalk, providing food to someone in need. We hope that those on the receiving end feel that love, that they think, "This person is thinking about me, cares about me, notices me, hears me, sees me."

Given through Action

Love is given through action. The grand narrative we've been exploring is a love story between the first and second characters. It's the story of God's active love for you and me. He set up a nation and provided them with land to enjoy and laws to obey. He set a foundation for the relationship that was built on freedom and trust. He sent Jesus as the ultimate expression of his love:

> *But God demonstrates his own love for us in this: While we were still sinners, Christ died for us. —Romans 5:8*

Love is not given as a feeling; it's demonstrated as action.

Throughout the story, God reminds us that he will be with us during times of pain, suffering, and loss. There are many who will stand with us during the good times. These are people who *enjoy* us. But the test of a relationship is who remains with us during the worst of times. These are the people who *love* us. Some people are not interested in a local sports team until the team makes a deep playoff run. Then they're excited and go buy a shirt they can wear at parties. Other fans follow and support the team through year after year of mediocrity. Those are the true fans. Those are the people who truly love the team.

Jesus' love shines brightest during the *rebuilding* seasons—during the difficult episodes of life. He declared that those who are poor in spirit, who mourn, who are meek, and who are persecuted will be blessed because they will come face-to-face with the active love of God.[2]

Through the worst moments of your previous episodes, God was there. He may not have stopped something awful from happening to you, but he didn't cause it. He was devastated by it as a parent is anguished by the suffering of a child.

God's active love for you is unconditional. In my marriage, there are times when my wife and I say to each other, "I love you, but I don't like you right now." In other words, I am disappointed or hurt by your behavior, but I will never stop loving you. Tami and I want to love each other that way because we know that's how God loves us. He may be disappointed by some of our decisions, but he will never stop actively loving us.

Received as a Feeling

On the receiving end, it's glorious to feel God's love.

While it's terrific to learn new information and discover the framework of God's story, it pales in comparison to feeling God's radiant love. Here's what your heart and mind can experience as you live out your current episode:

- When you woke up this morning, Jesus was with you, waiting to hear from you and spend time with you.
- When you felt alone, you were not.
- When you made a selfless or courageous decision, Jesus was cheering you on.
- When you made a poor decision, Jesus never abandoned you.

The early revolutionaries in the New Testament wrote things such as:

> *Rejoice always, pray continually, give thanks in all circumstances. —1 Thessalonians 5:16–18*

> *Let us continually offer to God a sacrifice of praise. —Hebrews 13:15*

They were always aware of God's presence. With every word they said or decision they made, they knew God was with them—not as a hovering supervisor but as a loving parent.

Years ago, I was jogging through a park in our neighborhood when I saw a four-year-old riding his bike with training wheels. His mom was twenty feet behind him. The boy stopped for no apparent reason, hopped off his bike, and went back to give his mom a knee-hug. He then ran back to his bike, hopped on, and continued his adventure through the park.

He gave his mom a mid-ride hug.

It's a very good day when we're aware of and thankful for God's presence all the time. Worship and prayer are about pausing in the middle of our current episode and giving God a mid-ride hug. It's about always being aware that he's with you. He hears what you say to the other bikers on the path. He sees when you go off the path and speed down the grassy hill.

Yes, you are sophisticated, intelligent, and complex. But in the eyes of God, the one who carved the Grand Canyon with his finger, you and I are simply riding bikes with training wheels. God is not impressed by us. He doesn't look at our accomplishments and think, "I'm sure glad they came along because I could not have handled that on my own." He actively loves us and wants us to feel that love. He wants us to be thankful for his presence, pause occasionally to give him a mid-ride hug, then hop on our bikes and enjoy the ride.

"Nevah"

Near the end of the movie *Batman Begins*, Alfred, the beloved butler, encourages Bruce Wayne when Bruce has reached his rock bottom.

Bruce: "I wanted to save Gotham. I failed."

Alfred: "Why do we fall, sir? So that we can learn to pick ourselves up."

Bruce: "You still haven't given up on me."

Alfred: "Nevah."

I'm sure it said "Never" in the script, but Michael Caine wonderfully made it sound like "Nevah."

We all have *delta moments* in life—painful realities resulting from what others have done to us or what we have done to ourselves. I have a friend who nearly died from alcoholism years ago. Like many, he joined AA, failed, joined again, then failed again. His first sponsor fired him. I didn't know that was possible, but apparently if you fail enough times, they're allowed to let you go. He got a second sponsor who said, "I will never give up on you. Never. God never gave up on me so who am I to give up on you?"

Some think God is like the first sponsor. He'll be available to a point, but eventually he'll turn his back on us. Fortunately, God is like the second sponsor. What Jesus modeled is a love that never gives up—that forgives not seven times but seventy-seven times.[3]

What happens when we are living with a secret in our current episode? We've grown calloused and we no longer care what God thinks about that part of our life. Will he ever walk away?

What happens when we recognize a repeating negative pattern in our life, and we choose to accept it? "That's just who I am. Take it or leave it. I'm bossy...I'm critical...I'm narcissistic...I'm grumpy." Will God eventually accept it as well?

What happens when we fall? Will God ever get to the point where he will no longer cheer for us? no longer pick us back up? Will he ever give up on us?

Nevah.

---

1. Another *Saturday Night Live* skit. This one is from the 1990s.
2. Matthew 5:3–12.
3. See Matthew 18:21–22. Jesus' words do not literally mean that godly forgiveness requires offering it seventy-seven times to someone. The number seven symbolizes "completeness" in the Bible. Therefore, it's reasonable to understand "seventy-seven times" as an unlimited number.

6.4 Next Episode

My wife prepares well for travel. She lays out clothes for each day in neatly folded piles. She has a just-in-case bag in the event things get stopped up or flow too freely. This bag also contains ear plugs, Band-Aids, and a bicycle-tire tube because you never know what's going to happen. She prepares well; I do not.

For my return to the States after my time in Africa, I arranged a one-week layover in Paris because I was right there and had the available time. It was a no-brainer (in more ways than one). It wasn't until I landed at Charles de Gaulle Airport with a suitcase full of wooden African animals, a backpack full of dirty clothes, and $100 in my pocket that I realized—I had no plans for where I was going to stay for a week in Paris. I remember sitting on a bench at the airport thinking, "Yikes! I am in, how you say...trouble!"

There's a huge difference between being prepared and not being prepared. A good coach prepares the athlete or the team for the next opponent. A good commander prepares the troops for the mission at hand. A good financial planner prepares a client for retirement.

Are you prepared for the next episodes of your life? Our previous episodes have been written, shot, edited, and archived. Our opportunity to write the next episode is now. We can either prepare for it or we can be unprepared—and it's always better to be prepared.

If you tell my wife I said that, I'll deny it.

Bell Curve

The Overall story is about your relationship with God; it's not about behavior management. It's not about doing what is right and avoiding what is wrong. But—there is a very practical benefit to living life with

Jesus as Lord. This life leads to the joy, the freedom, and the strength of making good decisions.

On the bell curve below, there are three phases to facing a temptation in your life. The first is the *prep* phase. This is what you do before the temperature rises. The second is the *moment* itself. This is when the temptation is at its hottest and is most difficult to resist. The third is the *response* phase. This is how others respond to you and how you feel about yourself. We ride this curve many times in life, often multiple times per day.

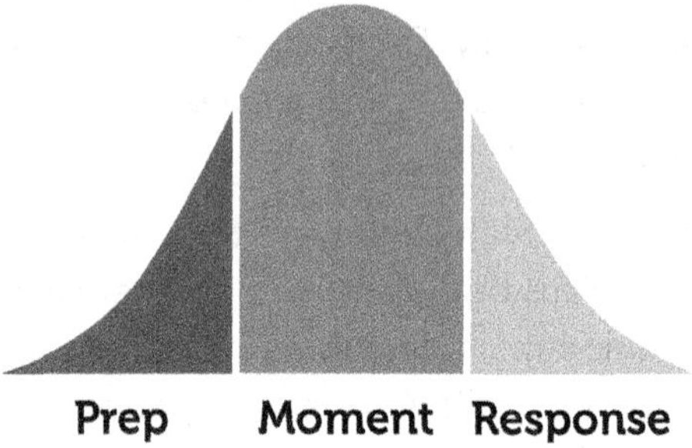

Let's work backwards through this. We addressed the *response* phase in Chapter 2.2. After we make poor decisions, the enemy brings shame and hopes we will question our value as well as God's interest in and love for us. This is where God's amazing grace shines. He instantly provides comfort and wants us to understand that he can never love us any less, no matter what we do. Hopefully, in this phase, we will seek his forgiveness and courageously make amends with those we have hurt.

The *moment* phase can be less than a minute, or it can endure over years of your life. It's when you come face-to-face with the power of your *control factors*. It's sitting at your computer and deciding which keys to press. It's holding the remote to the television and deciding what to watch. It's having potent information and deciding whether to share it, how to share it, and how much of it to share. It's enjoying privacy with someone you're attracted to, even though you know it's outside God's design for you.

This phase is when we are untethered from God's grand story and justifying our actions with thoughts such as "It's only once," or "I deserve a break," or "It's natural." In the *moment*, we choose the small story rather than the grand picture. We eat crumbs on the floor rather than sit at the table and enjoy the feast. We, like Esau, choose a bowl of stew over our family inheritance.[1]

The *response* is after the fact, and the *moment* is often too late. Therefore, it's the *prep* phase that is most significant. This is when we have the strength and ability to clarify values, identify boundaries, create restrictions, and commit to accountability. As Napoleon said, "The reason most people fail instead of succeed is they trade what they want most for what they want at the moment."

During the *prep* phase, we have the opportunity to prioritize what we "want most." We can picture our final episode and make decisions that head in that direction.

This is your life, are you who you want to be?

Training

We need training. That's why we go to church. That's the reason churches exist.

That's why we read the Bible, memorize the Scriptures, and learn sacred songs. So that we can be prepared for our upcoming episodes. In Chapter 3.4, I mentioned a profound experience I had with God where he redirected me from focusing on a young woman to focusing on his plan for my life. The message came through a song I was learning at that time, "I Lift My Eyes Up." The words echoed through my head as I was trying to collect myself. I was involved with a college ministry, and if I was not attending the weekly gatherings, I would not have recalled the lyrics, which are based on Psalm 121:

> *I lift my eyes up to the mountains—*
> *where does my help come from?*
> *My help comes from the Lord,*
> *the Maker of heaven and earth.* —*Psalm 121:1–2*

The reason we go to church, the reason we read the Bible on a regular basis, the reason we benefit from understanding the Overall story—is training. Right now, we are training for future episodes. We memorize the Scriptures because at that *moment* in the future, we won't have the opportunity to look something up. Do you instantly know what Jesus says about adultery, or gossip, or judging others? Do you know what the Bible has to say about *your* area of weakness—about your *control factors*?

Connecting with people at church is not about behavior management; it's about intimacy with them and God. It requires *ekklésia* (from Chapter 5.1), but it doesn't require a building. It's possible to be present at church but distant from anyone in the room. And it's possible to participate online, have daily encounters with God, and have meaningful interactions with others who are seeking to understand the grand story as well. It's not where you engage, it's how.

The reason we connect with a church is for training. We don't train during the week so we can be prepared to run the race on Sunday mornings. We train on Sunday mornings so we can run the race during the week. We gather because it's much more effective to train as a team than it is to train on our own—coaches and athletes understand this. We sing songs repeatedly so the lyrics will plant themselves in our brains and be accessible when we're in need. We listen to sermons so we can think differently about our relationships and upcoming decisions.

The pastor or priest is essentially your spiritual coach, and there are many different styles of coaching. Some yell at the players and inspire them with passion. Some have a terrific understanding of the game but are not skilled at transferring that information to the players. Some coaches are very kind but don't challenge the players to be their best. Others are more interested in being "liked" than getting the most out of the team. And there are even coaches who have the audacity to write a book they hope will assist both coaches and players.

Ahem.

The best thing you can do for the next episodes of your life is to train and prepare for them.

Wear the Armor

Paul, the former Christian-killer who became a spiritual coach to many new leaders throughout the Mediterranean, wrote the following about preparing for upcoming episodes:

> *Finally, be strong in the Lord and in his mighty power. Put on the full armor of God, so that you can take your stand against the devil's schemes. For our struggle is not against flesh and blood, but against the rulers, against the authorities, against the powers of this dark world and against the spiritual forces of evil in the heavenly realms. —Ephesians 6:10–12*

We previously viewed these words in Part II of the story (Violation). On the one hand, the existence of a "devil" who is scheming to sabotage your relationship with God is consistent throughout the Scriptures as well as church history. But, on the other hand, it sounds like kids' stuff. Christians can have intelligent conversations about politics, morality, science, sexuality, archeology, and theology. But as soon as we mention the "powers of this dark world" or the "spiritual forces of evil," we might as well give details of our recent alien abduction. Regardless of our culture's response to a "devil," we must decide if we believe he exists. The story we believe we're living in shapes how we live our lives. For me, I simply assume the enemy is at work. When my wife and I have a major fight over a minor issue, I don't assume it's nothing. When there's an unusual misunderstanding or a bad assumption, I try to pause and pray for guidance. Paul suggested we do more than that:

> *Therefore put on the full armor of God, so that when the day of evil comes, you may be able to stand your ground, and after you have done everything, to stand. —Ephesians 6:13*

The armor includes a *shield of faith* that protects us from *flaming arrows* that are the burning-hot areas of temptation. There's a *helmet of salvation* that guards our minds from doubting God's Overall story and his dominion over it. Among other items, there's a *sword of the Spirit* that Paul identified as the *word of God*. Again, we are wise to know what the Bible says instead of guessing or making assumptions.

Some people have significant armor—many years of sermons heard, Bible studies attended, and books read. But the armor is useless if it's piled up in the bottom of the closet. Others have little armor and feel insecure and ill-prepared for the next episodes *when the day of evil comes*. It's okay. You're doing the right thing now. You're learning, you're growing. You're building your armor, one ounce at a time.

Either way, God will not put the armor on for you. Every day we must *put on the full armor of God*. When the battle starts, when you're in the middle of the next episode of life, it's too late to put on the armor. When you're sitting on a bench at Charles de Gaulle Airport in Paris with $100 in your pocket, it's too late. When you've already had a few drinks, it's too late. When the two of you are alone in the bedroom, it's too late. When you receive the call that your loved one has died, it's too late. What can we do today to prepare ourselves for the next episode?

Use the Armor

In the exile story, Ahab was possibly the worst king in Israel's history, but I love what he said to the leader of an attacking army:

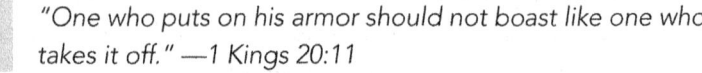

> *"One who puts on his armor should not boast like one who takes it off." —1 Kings 20:11*

That would make a great bumper sticker.

The king was saying that putting on armor is great, but it means nothing unless we're using it. The one who removes his armor has fought in battle and survived.

In Ephesians 6, Paul specifically identified six pieces of armor, but not all are for defense. God's plan is not for us to sit back and endure two thousand years of onslaught. Recall what Jesus said to Peter, the original leader of the church:

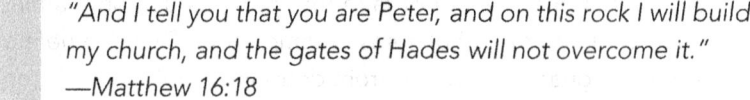

> *"And I tell you that you are Peter, and on this rock I will build my church, and the gates of Hades will not overcome it." —Matthew 16:18*

We don't put a sign around our dog's neck that says, "Beware of Gate." The purpose of a gate is to hold something back. A gate doesn't move; it doesn't advance. It's not an offensive threat; it's a line of defense. If the *gates of Hades* are impacted by the church, then the church is advancing.

Recall from Chapter 1.1 that there are two levels to the Overall story. There's a lower level that is the reality stage. It's the story you and I get to live in and our diligent efforts to understand life around us. Then there's the upper level, which is the supernatural stage where God and his angels combat Satan and his demons. When we remain in the lower level of the story, we're not advancing. We are no threat to the enemy because we're focused on comparing ourselves with one another and attaining the most impressive car, house, and reputation possible. At best we're in defense mode, but more likely we're not even aware of the battles going on around us. Our city is under siege and we're shopping for bathroom tile.

However, when we open our eyes to the reality of the second level, we begin to advance. We practice intentional parenting when our kids are struggling instead of waiting for an awkward phase to pass. We boldly discuss difficult topics with our spouse for the purpose of improving, not winning. We are profoundly honest about our *control factors* so we can rid them of their power. We understand that the enemy is at work, and we have had enough.

Any movement from the lower level to the upper level will meet resistance. *Gates of Hades* will be erected to slow us down, but they will not be able to stop us. We advance because the stakes are high. Your marriage, your relationships with your kids, your reputation, your character, and your peace of mind are worth it. Soldiers don't suit up to hide—they suit up to fight.

Become the Armor

Over time, the armor becomes who you are. The armor may feel clunky at first. It may feel weird to pray before you react, or to recall a Bible verse as a first step in decision-making. You may be concerned you're becoming Ned Flanders after many years of ignorant bliss as Homer Simpson.

But let me revisit *Iron Man* once again (perhaps over-referenced, but please stay with me). If you picture him in your mind, what does he look like? Is he wearing his red and gold armor? The first suit he created in a cave in Afghanistan was ridiculously clunky. Eventually, it seemed he could create an entire suit out of an accessory on his key-chain. Issues of "conservation of matter" notwithstanding, the armor became a natural part of his story. He went from *no armor* to *clunky armor* to *that's-who-he-is.*

When we spend enough time wearing and using the armor, we can become the armor. We can think about God's story first instead of starting with our fears and our desires. We can be regularly aware of what's happening on the upper level of the story while we enjoy what God provides for us on the lower level.

What can we do today to prepare ourselves for the next episode?

While writing this book, I have been part of a group of seven men who are boldly honest with one another. We have held nothing back, so we are past the point of shocking one another with our brokenness. When one of us trips, the other six are there to pick him up. I've taken steps to avoid my *control factor.* I have no games on my phone, and anyone in my family or my men's group can check it whenever they want. I choose to think in terms of "sobriety" rather than reduction. I don't want to give the enemy a foothold; I want to kick him in the teeth. The person I was in my previous episodes is not the person I am now. I'm an armor-bearing revolutionary who's ready to admit mistakes rather than hide them.

What do you think is most likely to derail you in your upcoming episodes? Whatever it is, don't respond to it—prepare for it. What is one piece of armor you can wear that will make you stronger? one step you can take to prepare? Perhaps you can be brutally honest with a friend you can trust. Or increase accountability on your electronic devices. Or stop spending time with a certain person or group of people. Or toss a large rock at your big-screen television. Or never again buy a certain item from a certain store.

What is one practical step you can take? Give your future self an immeasurable gift. You're more powerful right now, during the *prep* phase, than you will be in the heat of the *moment.* What can you do today to prepare yourself for the next episode of your life?

1. This refers to a brief story found in Genesis 25:29–34. Esau stormed into the tent famished. His brother, Jacob, was making stew and Esau asked for a bowl. Jacob said he would sell the stew for Esau's birthright—since Esau was the older of the two. Jacob may have been joking, but Esau took the deal anyway. Most expensive bowl of stew ever.

PART VII:
LAST WORDS

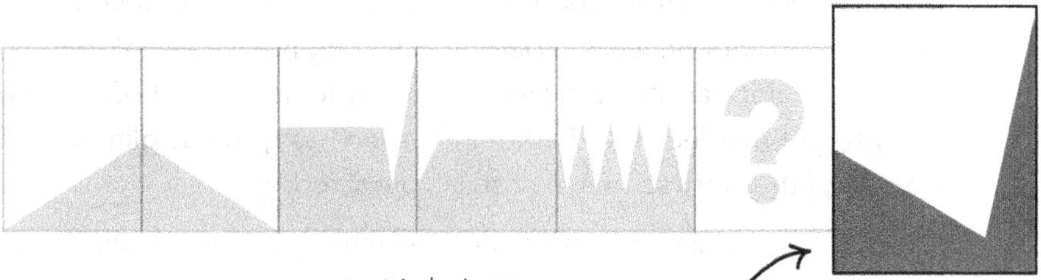

Last Words: it's gonna get worse before the glorious ending

Intro

We now enter wacky world.

The sections of the Bible that address the end of the story are known as "apocalyptic literature" and they are full of unsolved mystery and strange symbolism. Some people are obsessed with cracking the code and identifying when and how the world is going to end. So far, every guess prior to today's date has proven to be quite wrong. As G. K. Chesterton said, "Though [the author of Revelation] saw many strange monsters in his vision, he saw no creatures so wild as one of his own commentators."[1]

On the opposite end of the spectrum, others completely avoid this part of the story. They've decided it's too weird and seems to have nothing to do with real life. In the unlikely event Jesus returns during their lifetime, they imagine they'll figure out what to do at that point.

Hopefully, there's a provocative and relevant spot in the middle.

This part of the story is wacky because it's mostly reduced to conjecture. So far, we've been looking at actual events in human history. You get to decide whether the two-thousand-year-old evidence supports a resurrected Jesus or the greatest ruse the world has ever known. Some of the information is available and more will likely be discovered. But in *this* part of the story, all we have are hints, metaphors, and symbols. For this reason, we must enter the final section with great humility. Anyone who claims to have the end of the story all figured out should be handled with care.

The Book of Revelation is not a secret code or a cosmic puzzle. It's an extraordinary picture God has provided to prepare his loved ones for the end. That's what good parents do—they help their children get ready for major transitions in life. Is he ready for middle school? Is she ready to get married? Our Father in heaven has given us glimpses of the end of the story so that we can be prepared.

These three final chapters are not a summary of apocalyptic literature, and they will not come close to addressing all the questions that surface when we explore these writings in the Bible. Instead, they will address three phrases from the Book of Revelation that are important in terms of understanding how the Overall story ends.

1. From https://www.goodreads.com/quotes/381545-and-though-st-john-saw-many-strange-monsters-in-his, accessed May 27, 2022.

7.1 Worthy Is the Lamb

As the second of three main characters in this cosmic story, how do you think we humans are doing? We've been around for a long time. We've read about or watched many people make catastrophic mistakes. Are we getting any better? Are we becoming more like Jesus or drifting further away? What's your assessment?

When you look at the leaders of nations, the global economy, the reality and threat of war, the sex trade, the distribution of wealth, and the death of children in impoverished countries, how do you think we're doing?

Years ago, I officiated three funerals in one week. Joann had recently celebrated her thirtieth anniversary and was looking forward to thirty more years. Her death sent her husband into a tailspin of alcohol abuse that he has not yet recovered from. The second funeral was for Brian, a young husband who ended his battle with Lou Gehrig's disease. His death was a slow, painful process that attacked his nervous system and eventually shut down his lungs. Jennifer was the third funeral. She was a twenty-one-year-old fiancé who tripped at the top of a flight of stairs and broke her neck. I was with the grieving mom when she had to tell Jennifer's two younger brothers what happened. Before she spoke, she looked up at me and whispered, "A mother shouldn't have to do this."

If the Christian story is one of victory, where Jesus died on the cross and then conquered death by rising from the grave, why does it often feel as if we're still losing? Why is there still pain, and suffering, and death? If Satan is no match for God, then why is Satan still running rampant here on earth?

It's obvious that hell and its captain are still wreaking havoc. So it's reasonable to ask: What the "hell" is going on?

Three Main Characters

God, Satan, and people remain the three main characters through the *Last Words* of the story. In the Book of Revelation there is plenty of mysterious symbolism and admitted ambiguity, but there is tremendous clarity regarding the fate of the big three. *God wins. Satan loses. And people have a choice to make.*

The Book of Revelation could be summed up with the two words *God wins*. In the end, God is victorious. Revelation was written by a man named John while he was exiled on the island of Patmos in the Mediterranean Sea. It's a vision of what the end of the story will look like. Remember, Jesus is God, and he appeared to John in the Book of Revelation, saying,

> *"Do not be afraid. I am the First and the Last. I am the Living One; I was dead, and now look, I am alive for ever and ever! And I hold the keys of death and Hades."*
> *—Revelation 1:17–18*

It's the beginning of an incredible vision centered around the promise that Jesus will return and conquer every manifestation of evil.

God wins, and *Satan loses*. There's little ambiguity regarding the fate of the antagonist in the story:

> *And the devil, who deceived them, was thrown into the lake of burning sulfur, where the beast and the false prophet had been thrown. They will be tormented day and night for ever and ever. —Revelation 20:10*

This isn't wishful thinking. It isn't one interpretation of a possible way the story will end. The mystery in the Book of Revelation is about the details, not the outcome of the main characters. Getting thrown into the lake of burning sulfur is really bad. Jesus will return and obliterate Satan.

God wins. Satan loses. And *God's people have a choice to make*. This includes you and me and all of humanity, the objects of his love and affection. We will ultimately choose one side or the other in the cosmic contest between God and his adversary. We will explore what this means in the next chapter.

If God wins and Satan loses, why do we continue to suffer in this life? The reason is that we live in the period between Jesus' first and second comings. The end result of the war has been decided, but the fighting is not yet over.

The fate of Germany and the Axis powers in World War II was determined by the American, British, Canadian, and other Allied troops that invaded Normandy in 1944. The battle on the beaches of northern France was fierce and historic, but little seemed to change elsewhere in Europe at that time. Most of the continent was still under Nazi control and the concentration camps were still going about their horrific business. While the D-Day invasion sealed the outcome of World War II, the war was far from over. The Battle of the Bulge would follow, and it saw the loss of more American troops than any other operation during the war. The Allied forces won the victory at Normandy and ensured the end of the war, but the battles were still raging.

In a similar way, the Overall Christian story holds the same two realities: God wins *and* the war is still raging. If we only embrace the first part and ignore the second, we will assume that following Jesus means everything will be wonderful. Our kids will thank us regularly for loving them enough to provide meaningful chores and clear boundaries; our boss will reward us for our unseen, extra efforts; our hair will get thicker; and our belly will get tighter.

However, if we focus on the spiritual war that is raging and doubt God's victory in the end, we're likely to get depressed and lose hope. Your opportunity to experience both purpose and joy in this world depends on your willingness to embrace both parts: God wins *and* the war is still raging.

In Jesus' words to his disciples,

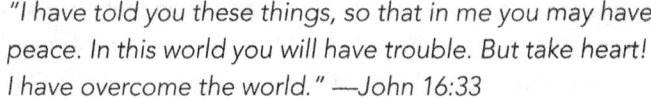

> *"I have told you these things, so that in me you may have peace. In this world you will have trouble. But take heart! I have overcome the world." —John 16:33*

The Scroll

John's Revelation uses the symbol of a scroll to describe Jesus' victory. We use books; they used scrolls. The scroll was rolled up and locked with seven seals like the soft wax marked by a signet ring. The seals represent the destructive work of the enemy. The first four are known as the *Four Horsemen of the Apocalypse*, which sounds appropriately menacing. They are conquest, war, famine, and death. The fifth seal represents those who have died for their faith and the sixth is about natural disasters. The seventh seal opens a whole new list of earthly brokenness.

The scroll is like a title deed to the universe. If it remains closed, Satan will maintain power and the war will rage on. John was not just *recording* a vision—he was experiencing it:

> *I wept and wept because no one was found who was worthy to open the scroll or look inside. —Revelation 5:4*

This is when the story gets really cool. There is one, and only one, who is worthy to open the scroll. It's like Excalibur, the sword, waiting for King Arthur or Mjölnir, the hammer, waiting for Thor, the god of thunder.

> *Then one of the elders said to me, "Do not weep! See, the Lion of the tribe of Judah, the Root of David, has triumphed. He is able to open the scroll and its seven seals." —Revelation 5:5*

God wins. The seven seals will be broken, and suffering will come to an end because there is one who is worthy. In the upper level of the story, there are armies of angels. They're not chubby babies with fluffy wings; they're enormous warriors. Imagine a hundred million of them chanting,

> *"Worthy is the Lamb...!" —Revelation 5:12*

A *hundred million* of them.

For just a moment, pause your brain's efforts to make sense of the story and its symbols. Let the voices of the chanting angels send chills up your spine. This is the climax of the entire story. It's Luke Skywalker firing his proton torpedoes into the thermal exhaust port. It's Frodo tossing the ring into the fires of Mount Doom. It's Tony Stark snapping his fingers.

Worthy is the Lamb!

The Lamb

Revelation 5:5 is the one and only time in the Scriptures that Jesus is referred to as the *Lion of Judah*. Twenty-eight times he's referred to as the Lamb. It's difficult for us to wrap our minds around the power of a lamb. If C. S. Lewis had written a story titled *The Lamb, the Witch and the Wardrobe,* it probably would have sold fewer copies.

A lamb is a very docile animal. They were certainly raised to become valuable sheep, but also at times were treated as pets by children. It would be like us thinking of a puppy or a kitten. Our family has a cockapoo named Daisy. It's difficult for me to imagine any ancestor of hers surviving in the wild. She chases bunnies, but she couldn't come within twenty feet of one—even if it was a baby bunny with a wounded leg. If I swat a fly and it's flopping around on the ground, she *might* be able to finish it off. If she was home alone when a burglar entered our house, she would roll over on her back as if to say, "You can take whatever you want, but before you leave could you please rub right here on my belly?"

The angels chant "Worthy is the Lamb," not "Worthy is the Lion." Abraham's son, Isaac, asked his dad, "Where's the lamb?" as they were walking up Mount Moriah. The Passover story in the Book of Exodus required God's people to mark their doors with the blood of a lamb. When John the Baptist saw Jesus, he exclaimed, "There's the Lamb of God!" A lamb was a perfect, sweet, lovable animal. It was a powerful sacrifice because it beautifully contrasted against the ugliness of sin.

Jesus was beautiful toward others. He was loving, caring, forgiving, and gracious. He was the ultimate sacrifice for the repulsive sin of all humanity.

> *Then I saw a Lamb, looking as if it had been slain, standing at the center of the throne. —Revelation 5:6*

The hero in the final battle of the story of humanity is a sweet little lamb covered in his own blood.

The Dragon

In stark contrast, Satan is referred to as the great *dragon*.

Those who dismiss the Christian story tend to mock the idea of Satan, but many remain oddly interested in the provocative images in the Book of Revelation, such as the beast, the number of the beast (666), the mark of the beast, and of course, the dragon:

> *Then another sign appeared in heaven: an enormous red dragon with seven heads and ten horns and seven crowns on its heads. Its tail swept a third of the stars out of the sky and flung them to the earth. The dragon stood in front of the woman who was about to give birth, so that it might devour her child the moment he was born. —Revelation 12:3–4*

These images are all about power—something humanity has always been interested in. God used power in the early stages of history to get the attention of his people. He flooded the earth, parted the Red Sea, and scorched an altar on Mount Carmel.[1] When Jesus came along, he wanted to heal hearts, but people were most impressed by his demonstrations of power. Even the disciples were confused and desired elevated positions alongside Jesus. In the story of the church, a constant desire has been power, and the constant result has been brokenness.

We have always been and continue to be drawn to power. Hollywood and pop culture lap up all the dark and vivid symbols from the last book of the Bible. But there's little pop culture interest in the *Lamb*—the one who ends up being victorious over all.

Lamb versus Dragon

The end of the story is a cosmic battle between God and Satan, represented by a lamb and a dragon—a battle between the most gentle and innocent creature imaginable and the most ferocious and vile monster one could envision. It's like a battle between a puppy laying on his back and an *enormous red dragon with seven heads*. It's far more extreme than David versus Goliath. The battle between lamb and dragon is a battle between sacrifice and power.

And in God's grand story, sacrifice always wins.

The hidden power of sacrifice is that it *can't* lose.

Much great fiction is grounded in the idea of sacrifice. We are drawn to it. In an epic series of novels titled *Red Rising*, author Pierce Brown brings to life a character named Darrow, the leader and hero. He's faced with a dilemma because a fellow warrior named Tactus has violated one of his own people. If Darrow is too harsh as leader, he'll lose half of his troops. If he's too merciful, he'll lose the other half. He spares Tactus's life but whips him twenty times for his crime. Then he removes his own shirt and tells Tactus to give him twenty-five lashes back. Because of his own beating, Tactus is weak and so are his lashes. So Darrow commands his strongest warrior to step in and finish the job. When the gruesome deed is done, Darrow stands up with his mutilated back and says to his troops, "Anyone who does anything vile…will have to whip me like this in front of the entire army."[2]

Scenes like this are deeply moving because we are made in the image of God. The power of sacrifice is written on the human heart, and when we see it, something is stirred within us. It could be Severus Snape's concealed protection of Harry Potter, or Anna's willingness to shield Elsa from Hans's sword in *Frozen*, or the Terminator's final thumbs-up as he's lowered into molten steel. It could be sacrifice for a nation, or a family member, or even for a stranger. Heroes put someone else above themselves; villains do the opposite. Whether or not we're ready to do it in our own lives, something deep inside us is touched when we watch even fictional sacrifice.

But Jesus isn't fictional. He said it:

> *"Greater love has no one than this: to lay down one's life for one's friends." —John 15:13*

Then he modeled it.

He didn't defeat his enemies—he died for them. That's how he conquered evil:

> *They triumphed over [Satan] by the blood of the Lamb. —Revelation 12:11*

This is not a side issue. It's not a nugget found deep in the last words of the Bible. It is the Overall story. The battle that started in the garden of Eden and had its greatest triumph on a cross in Jerusalem will end in a showdown between the Lamb and the dragon. It's a battle that requires us to choose sides. As nations, cities, families, and individuals, will we align ourselves with the dragon and continue to seek power? Or will we align with the Lamb and choose to sacrifice?

> *After this I looked, and there before me was a great multitude that no one could count, from every nation, tribe, people and language, standing before the throne and before the Lamb.*
> *—Revelation 7:9*

Of course, we choose Jesus over Satan. That's an easy decision. And John's vision paints a glorious picture of a *great multitude* siding with the slaughtered Lamb over the mighty dragon.

But how often do we choose power over sacrifice?

Worthy—victorious—triumphant—is the Lamb.

---

1. 1 Kings 18:16–46.
2. Pierce Brown, *Red Rising* (New York: Random House, 2013), 303.

7.2 Book of Life

I didn't focus solely on academics when I was in graduate school. While my colleagues were debating theology in the lounge, I was exploring the extracurricular activities of the undergraduate program. Perhaps I wasn't quite ready to be "old" or "mature" yet.

The drama department advertised auditions for a clever whodunit play. I had years of practice being a disruption in classrooms, but very little experience performing on an actual stage. At this time in my life, I was in a perpetual "yes" position to whatever opportunity God set in front of me.

Everything about the audition was new to me. The play was British, so we all had to display our accent skills—and what North Americans think they *can't* pull off an excellent British accent? We all read a few sections from the play, then each of us was to perform a prepared monologue.

Excuse me—a what?

All the drama students had several monologues to choose from. The only thing I could think of was Jack Nicholson's final speech in *A Few Good Men*. Yes, I knew the whole thing without preparation.

"Son, we live in a world that has walls. And those walls need to be guarded by men with guns…."

Three days later, the director would post the cast list, which identifies who got what part. Have you ever waited for such a list—perhaps something you auditioned for or a team you were hoping to make? It's nerve wracking. Your name on that list will be a significant factor in your level of joy over the next two to three months. That list shapes the next episode of your story.

My name was not on the cast list. I wanted to ask the director why, but I decided against it—perhaps I knew that I *can't handle the truth*.

In this chapter we'll explore the reality of the *book of life*—a cast list for eternity.

Second Character

The fate of the protagonist and antagonist are set: God wins, Satan loses. But the fate of the second character (us—at least those of us who are still drawing breath) has yet to be determined.

This should make sense to us because we're all a blend of good and evil. Everything good in the world is God, and everything evil is Satan. We're not perfectly one or the other. We find ourselves somewhere in the middle, which is a place that will not exist in eternity. In the end, we will either side with good or with evil. We will either find our name written in the book of life or we will not.

Many don't like this plan. Many don't like the clarity of black and white, and prefer the gray in between. How could a loving God allow the existence of hell? There must be a loophole. There must be something we don't understand. As long as I stay on the good side of center, everything should be fine, right?

These thoughts are reasonable, but immeasurably risky.

The Book of Revelation was written to seven specific churches, and it begins with words of encouragement and challenge for each. These seven messages from Jesus to seven actual churches told them exactly what he was looking for.

Wouldn't that be great? Isn't that what we want from our spouses and bosses? To give us specific feedback that we can work on rather than "I don't feel loved" or "You're just not a good fit"?

What a gift Jesus was offering—an evaluation. In what ways were these churches leaning toward the light and in what ways were they fading into darkness? To the seventh church, Jesus said,

> *"You are neither cold nor hot. I wish you were either one or the other! So, because you are lukewarm—neither hot nor cold—I am about to spit you out of my mouth. You say, 'I am rich; I have acquired wealth and do not need a thing.' But you do not*

> *realize that you are wretched, pitiful, poor, blind and naked."*
> *—Revelation 3:15–17*

In the end, there's no lukewarm. There's either hot or cold. Like these churches, each one of us will be evaluated. We'll have reason to merit both encouragement and challenge, but are we leaning toward the light or fading into darkness? Are we *in* or are we *out*? Is our name on the list or not? How can we know?

Assumption

Our first response might be to gaze upon Tim Tebow's eye-black. You may recall that he had a verse cited in white ink under his eyes. It's the same verse many have displayed at highly publicized sporting events:

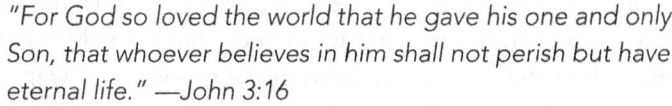

> *"For God so loved the world that he gave his one and only Son, that whoever believes in him shall not perish but have eternal life." —John 3:16*

It's the most famous verse in the Bible for a reason. We don't need to *do* anything. We simply need to believe. Absolutely.

But—there's an assumption with that belief.

Imagine you're the general manager of a professional hockey team.

(I'm Canadian, bear with me....)

You're prepared to add an incredibly talented and experienced new player. This is the kind of guy who can lead a team to win the Stanley Cup. In an interview, you ask the player if he believes in your team and he, of course, replies that he does. There's an assumption with that belief—that he will show up for practice and inspire the young players. He won't rest on what he accomplished with his previous team, but he'll strive to improve himself. He won't be satisfied with "good enough" and will continue to seek excellence. There is an assumption that is attached to this player and his new team.

Whoever believes in him from John 3:16 is not a low bar. It's a gracious start of a life committed to sacrificially loving others. Belief in Jesus assumes respect for his commands. Some call it "evidence of faith." James, the brother of Jesus, wrote, "Faith without works is dead."[1] It's critical to understand the assumption that comes with our faith in Jesus because, in the end, many will be surprised. Jesus warns,

> *"Wide is the gate and broad is the road that leads to destruction, and many enter through it. But small is the gate and narrow the road that leads to life, and only a few find it."* *—Matthew 7:13–14*

Good-hearted people will not stumble into heaven by the grace of God. Only a few will find it. *Only a few.* Fortunately, Jesus *is* the gate[2] and he has provided clarity regarding the assumptions that come with our faith.

Olivet Discourse

Part VII (Last Words) is not a summary of the Book of Revelation. It's a quick peek at some of the key phrases that help us understand how the Overall story will come to an end. There are clues in Part II (Violation) from some of the writings of the prophets, as well as Part IV (Revolution) in a few of Paul's letters. Perhaps the most fascinating verses are found in Part III, in Matthew's version of the story of Jesus. Here we find two chapters that are known as the "Olivet Discourse" because Jesus spoke these words at the Mount of Olives. These are Jesus' words, so there's no wiggle room to say they were "for a certain group of people at a certain time." He said,

> *"Two men will be in the field; one will be taken and the other left. Two women will be grinding with a hand mill; one will be taken and the other left." —Matthew 24:40–41*

Brilliant men and women have debated for centuries what will happen in the end. In these verses, Jesus provided details about his followers who still walk this earth being removed from their current life at his return. Some call this event the "rapture," and there are different opinions about a time of "tribulation" and a "millennium" of time to accompany it. In this book, I have chosen not to summarize these perspectives nor persuade toward a particular one. I'll leave that to authors who debated theology in the lounge at their graduate school. Instead, I have chosen to focus on the essential elements of the story: Do we acknowledge Jesus as the one who is worthy and are we prepared for his return?

The Sheep and the Goats

The Olivet Discourse concludes with a sobering story. Jesus presented an image of the King separating people as a shepherd separates the sheep from the goats. This was standard practice for a shepherd during feeding, because sheep are mild and goats are aggressive. If you want to traumatize your children, fill their little palms with pellets and put them in a pen full of goats. I know from experience how this can turn a lovely day at a petting zoo into a screaming nightmare.

The King congratulates the sheep because they cared for him when he was hungry, thirsty, sick, and in prison. The sheep were excited to please the King, but were confused because they were unaware that the King was ever in need. The King replies,

> *"Truly I tell you, whatever you did for one of the least of these brothers and sisters of mine, you did for me."* —Matthew 25:40

This is a beautiful response from a King who needs nothing, to his people who cared for others and expected no credit. Jesus was not waxing philosophical here. He provided six practical examples: the hungry, the thirsty, the lonely, the unclothed, the sick, and the prisoners. These aren't the magic six—I'm sure Jesus could have listed a hundred different needs. His point was that his command to "love one another" was not a suggestion. It's not a bonus activity for those who are super-followers. He then shook the foundation of our theology by addressing the goats:

> *"Whatever you did not do for one of the least of these, you did not do for me."* —Matthew 25:45

The grand story is not just about sin management or the absence of bad. Jesus assumed the presence of good. In the end, it won't be enough to say, "I didn't *take* food or clothing away from those in need. I didn't kick a stranger out of my home or wrongfully imprison someone." If you have a relationship with Jesus (which was the focus of Part III), then it will change you. It will affect you. If you're not changed or affected, then there's no relationship. A goat who knows the story of Jesus is still a goat.

This should rattle your bones.

Judgment

My oldest son played trumpet in school. During a middle school concert, my seat provided me with a line of sight to watch all four trumpet players at the same time—three of my son's bandmates, then Gordon at the end. My son and two of the other players were moving their fingers in unison and taking breaths together. But the young boy closest to me must have had a unique sheet of music. He had a very different finger pattern, breathed at different times, and took multiple opportunities to wave at his adoring fans in the audience.

He was *pretending* to play.

He wasn't becoming a trumpet player. He was only appearing to be one when people were looking. When it comes to the names of the *sheep* listed in the book of life, there will be no pretending. No loopholes. No back door. Let's return to the Book of Revelation:

> *I saw the dead, great and small... —Revelation 20:12*

The CEOs and the homeless. The professors and the dropouts. Those who fear justice and those who long for it.

> *...standing before the throne, and books were opened. Another book was opened, which is the book of life. The dead were judged according to what they had done as recorded in the books.... Anyone whose name was not found written in the book of life was thrown into the lake of fire.*
> *—Revelation 20:12, 15*

No pretending. No loopholes. No back door.

There.

Will.

Be.

Judgment.

Those who don't know the Overall story might think that God is bluffing. Those who are unfamiliar with the prolific warnings before the exile and that God did what he said he would do might read this chapter on the book of life and think, "There's no way."

"There's no way the gate is narrow and that only a few will find eternal life. There's no way followers will be caught off-guard and discover they are goats. There's no way Jesus will separate those who had an active faith from those who had an inactive faith. There's no way."

Are you sure?

"Maybe—hopefully—I guess we'll just have to see."

Picture in your mind the most precious people in your life right now—your parents, spouse, kids, friends. If they were borrowing your vehicle to take a trip to the mountains, and your mechanic said your brakes have a fifty percent chance of failing, is that enough? Would you get the brakes fixed before the trip, or would you send them off and think, "Maybe—hopefully—I guess we'll just have to see"?

How confident are you that Jesus is the crux of the story? That he rose again, that he will one day return, and that he is worthy to open the scroll? How confident are you that our faith in Jesus has an active assumption connected to it? Are you willing to bet your life on it? Are you willing to bet the most precious people in your life on it? The Bible celebrates Abraham's faith because even though he didn't know the whole story, he was willing to put his son on the altar. He was willing to bet all he had.

If you're a betting person, how much should you bet on Jesus?

The correct answer is—all of it.

Everything. Every hope, every dream, every doubt, every dark secret. Everything. Sometimes we go halfway in and say, "Maybe Jesus, maybe not—I just want to keep my bases covered and my options open—maybe be faithful on Sunday, maybe unfaithful on Saturday." When we hold something back, we're driving through treacherous mountains with brakes that could fail at any moment. Preparing for the end of the story means we *know* our name is written in the book of life because we *know* Jesus. It's not, "Maybe—hopefully—I guess we'll have to see."

How much should you bet on Jesus? The correct answer is—all of it.

When you choose to be one of the Twelve, get to know Jesus, and do what he says, you're putting it all in. All of it.

As a reminder, Matthew 24 and 25 are referred to as the "Olivet Discourse."

How much should we be willing to bet on Jesus?

Olivet!

1. James 2:26 (New King James Version).
2. John 10:9.

7.3 New Heaven and Earth

In 1982, Prince imagined partying like it was the end of the millennium. The last two chapters of the Bible relate John's vision of the party at the end of the grand story.

And it's gonna be big.

Huge.

> *He who was seated on the throne said, "I am making everything new!" —Revelation 21:5*

The closing ceremonies will be spectacular. All parts of the Overall story will come together as God creates a "new heaven and a new earth," which was foreshadowed during the exile through the prophet Isaiah:

> *In the last days*
> *the mountain of the LORD's temple will be established*
> *as the highest of the mountains;*
> *it will be exalted above the hills,*
> *and all nations will stream to it. —Isaiah 2:2*

This is Mount Moriah—the same mountain where Abraham was willing to sacrifice his son and Jesus was willing to sacrifice himself. The place of sacrifice will be transformed by the arrival of a heavenly city:

> *I saw the Holy City, the new Jerusalem, coming down out of heaven from God, prepared as a bride beautifully dressed for her husband. —Revelation 21:2*

There will also be a connection with the beautiful garden of Eden from the beginning of the grand story:

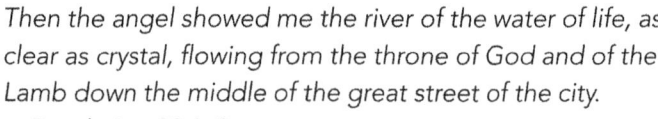

> *Then the angel showed me the river of the water of life, as clear as crystal, flowing from the throne of God and of the Lamb down the middle of the great street of the city.*
> *—Revelation 22:1–2*

Indescribable

Revelation 21 and 22 attempt to put into words what the indescribable end of the story is going to look like. They tell of streets of gold, gates made of massive pearls, and no need for a sun because the glory of God will provide endless light.

But what if that description doesn't sound appealing? Will we be singing songs all day? listening to choirs? Will we be reunited with our spouse? Will we *have* to be reunited with our spouse?

Ha.

C. S. Lewis cleverly and aggressively addressed these concerns:

> There is no need to be worried by facetious people who try to make the Christian hope of "Heaven" ridiculous by saying they do not want "to spend eternity playing harps". The answer to such people is that if they cannot understand books written for grown-ups, they should not talk about them. All the scriptural imagery (harps, crowns, gold, etc.) is, of course, a merely symbolical attempt to express the inexpressible.... People who take these symbols literally might as well think that when Christ told us to be like doves, He meant that we were to lay eggs.[1]

There are some life experiences that cannot be fully captured in words.

For example, I love ice cream. I'm not an ice cream snob—I love all sorts of flavors and all levels of quality. I love the hardness of cold ice cream as it resists my impatient spoon. I love watching it relax and warm up to me—first the edges, then the soft underbelly. I love the symphony of flavors that play their parts perfectly in the auditorium that is my mouth and throat. I love how the coldness soothes any remaining heat and anger from my day. Each bite is like a mini-celebration, skating around the inside of my mouth holding the Stanley Cup high in the air after a hard-fought victory.

You may or may not be stirred by my non-hyperbolic description of ice cream. After all, these are just words, an attempt to describe something that must be experienced. John's words that describe the new heaven and new earth are not meant to be dissected. They're meant to assure us that it will be magnificent.

Glimpse of Glory

God has a sensational party planned for the love of his life (second character) at the end of the story. Satan wants nothing more than to crash that party. He wants us to believe that this broken, painful world is as good as it gets.

Please don't believe that lie.

Jesus invited us to pray that we would see moments "on earth as it is in heaven."[2] When I was growing up in Edmonton, Canada, there was a worship event in the city called Glimpse of Glory. At the time, I didn't appreciate the beauty of that phrase. In a world bombarded with selfishness, deception, and struggles for power, there are beautiful moments we get to experience that reflect the glory of heaven.

In his Letter to the Romans, Paul wrote,

> *The whole creation has been groaning as in the pains of childbirth right up to the present time. —Romans 8:22*

All of creation is longing for the explosive release of the new heaven and new earth. In the meantime, we see an elbow pushing against the inside of the belly or a foot trying to kick its way out. These are glimpses or hints of what is to come. These are moments when people love others as Jesus commanded. When a child boldly sticks up for the new kid who does not yet fit in. When the smile of a terminally ill patient is the brightest one in the room. When a lukewarm believer goes on a mission trip and returns blazing hot. When people are prioritized over productivity. When a small act of kindness brings a stranger to tears.

These are glimpses of glory. Hints of heaven. These are the great moments of life. Not the successes and the accolades we tend to obsess over, but the days when heaven comes down and we get to taste it and see how wondrous it is.

It's like the trailer of a great movie—we love it and we want more. It's like an appetizer before a great feast; the bacon-wrapped scallops are sensational, but they're just a taste of what is to come.

Life on earth is not capable of full-time heaven. We see glimpses of greatness—a memorable moment, a perfect day, an amazing season of life—but then we snap back to non-heaven. The anger returns. The comparison sneaks in. The boredom resurfaces. During our lives, we are gifted with glimpses of glory; in the end, it is all we will see.

Faith, Hope, and Love

We occasionally get a taste of heaven because God made us, and he understands what we need. The second main character in the Overall story desperately needs *hope.*

In Chapter 4.3 of this book, we briefly looked at Paul's revolutionary Letters to the Corinthians and the famous "love chapter" found in 1 Corinthians 13. At the end of this short chapter, he wrote,

> *And now these three remain: faith, hope and love. But the greatest of these is love. —1 Corinthians 13:13*

Faith.

Hope.

And love.

Faith is what we believe. It's sometimes referred to as a "faith system" or a "belief system." It's the intellectual, emotional, and spiritual position we land on regarding God, ourselves, and others. It's the grand story we believe we're living in. We all have faith in something—the issue is what we have faith in and the depth of that faith.

Let me jump to Paul's third word: *love*. It truly is the "greatest of these" three. It's the whole point of the story. At the beginning of the "love chapter," Paul wrote,

> *If I...can fathom all mysteries and all knowledge, and if I have a faith that can move mountains, but do not have love, I am nothing. —1 Corinthians 13:2*

Life is meaningless without love. Our plans, talents, decisions, resources, and relationships are dust in the wind if they are not somehow connected to loving others. As we discovered in the previous chapter (7.2), the final judgement of humankind will be based on whether our faith in Jesus led us to take his words seriously. We are here to get to know Jesus and do what he says. We are here to "love one another."

The link between *faith* and *love* is *hope*. Hope is what carries us when love isn't working. When people are not responding well. When we try to the take the high road by listening rather than defending. When we courageously confess our responsibility in a conflict but get nothing in return. When we sacrificially provide for others and receive no credit or appreciation. Hope is the reminder that love is always the greatest, even when it doesn't look like it.

An extreme example is Corrie ten Boom's experience in Ravensbrück, a German concentration camp during World War II. She smuggled a Bible into her barracks and had forbidden worship "services" she referred to as "little previews of heaven."[3] Glimpses of glory in an environment that was the antithesis of love. She later recalled,

> I would look about us as Betsie [Corrie's sister] read, watching the light leap from face to face. More than conquerors.... It was not a wish. It was a fact. We knew it, we experienced it minute by minute—poor, hated, hungry. We are more than conquerors. Not "we shall be." We are! Life in Ravensbrück took place on two separate levels, mutually impossible. One, the observable, external life, grew every day more horrible. The other, the life we lived with God, grew daily better, truth upon truth, glory upon glory."[4]

Two separate levels. The upper level was the supernatural reality that God was present, aware, and faithful. The lower level was Corrie's horrific imprisonment in which she clung to the hope that believers are more than conquerors.

Humans are desperate for hope. It's commonly understood that lottery ticket sales are much higher among the poor. Those who don't have money are more likely to waste it on a chance to win the big prize. It's not that poor people are ignorant and don't understand how much the odds are against them. It's not that they are incapable of understanding the math. They're simply willing to spend $20 so that during the time between the purchase of the ticket and the calling of the numbers, they can have hope.

Humanity desperately needs hope.

Faith is the belief system; it's the story we believe we're living in. *Hope* is what keeps faith alive; it is fueled by glimpses of glory. And *love* is the ultimate result.

Last Words

Last words are often the most memorable.

> "Louis, I think this is the beginning of a beautiful friendship."
> —*Casablanca*

> "Roads? Where we're going, we don't need roads."
> —*Back to the Future*

In arguments, we rarely hear someone say, "I've said all I needed to say—I'll let you have the last word." Do you know Jesus' final words in the Scriptures? He used a four-word phrase three times in the last chapter of the Bible. The phrase is like the one made famous by Arnold Schwarzenegger in the *Terminator* movies.

Go ahead and look it up in Revelation 22:20. Jesus' last words are words of hope.

In one sense, these words are puzzling. If my dad told me he'd "be right back" and didn't return for two thousand years, I would likely feel a significant level of abandonment.

But my trust in Jesus assures me there's wisdom in his last words. If parents were to leave their teenager home alone for the weekend, would it be better to say "We'll be back soon," or "We'll be back on Monday at 7 PM"? Wise parents want their child to know they can return at any moment.

Are you ready for Jesus to walk through your front door and say, "Time's up"? Is there a broken relationship in your life that needs mending? Is there someone you need to reach out to? care for?

forgive? Is there a deep desire God placed in you that you have not yet pursued? Are you prepared to explain why an assignment from God has been *sitting on your desk* for years? Is there something you need to build, create, write, or start?

What are you waiting for?

Are you ready for the Lamb of God to return and verify his role in the grand story? Are you prepared to gaze upon his blood-stained face and thank him for his sacrifice, or will you remain confused about the "archaic" and "irrelevant" Christian story? Will you be excited about the end of the story and confident your name is written in the book of life? Will you run to him with familiar love, or will you cower with regretful fear?

Are you ready for the King of Kings to rule the new heaven and new earth? Are you ready for the glimpses and hints to turn into never ending joy? Are you ready for a Kingdom in which there will be no more tears, no more death or mourning or pain?

There are no words to describe the beauty of the new heaven and the new earth. But the party at the end of the Overall story will be orchestrated by the one who made us, knows us, and loves us more than we can imagine. It will be spectacular. And though I have no biblical support, I am confident there will be ice cream. Lots of ice cream.

---

1. C. S. Lewis, *Mere Christianity* (New York: HarperCollins, 1952), 137.
2. Matthew 6:10.
3. Corrie ten Boom, *The Hiding Place* (Grand Rapids: Baker Publishing, 2006), 222.
4. Ibid., 215.

Epilogue

As a framework for God's grand story, the seven parts of *Overall* are not the answer. They are not a solution to a cosmic puzzle. God is way too vast and mysterious for that.

The prophet Ezekiel had a majestic vision of God. After his attempt to put the vision into words, he wrote,

> *This was the appearance of the likeness of the glory of the Lord. —Ezekiel 1:28*

In other words, "All that I just wrote—It's not even close."

When J. J. Abrams was ten years old, he was enthralled by magic and his dad bought him a "mystery box" full of tricks. All it had on the outside of the box was a big question mark. That unopened box apparently remains in his office to this day because the mystery is actually more appealing than what's inside.

That which is a mystery is not *less* than that which is understood. Sometimes it's much greater. Parts of God and his story are not to be figured out; they are simply to be enjoyed.

This book is dedicated to my sage mother-in-law, whose favorite verse in the Bible is,

> *The secret things belong to the Lord our God, but the things revealed belong to us and to our children forever, that we may follow all the words of this law. —Deuteronomy 29:29*

There are *secret things* none of us are to understand, categorize, or figure out. And that's more than okay.

Nonetheless, in my journey with God I have found it extremely helpful to take the lumber of stories and assemble a framework in order to understand and appreciate him more. Every sermon, book, podcast,

Bible reading, and life experience fits somewhere in the *Overall* framework. It allows me to see the order of events and how stories build on one another. It also helps me identify ideas and thoughts that do not fit with God's grand story.

If you have a different structure that helps you understand the grand story, terrific. I hope something in this book strengthens that framework. But if you don't currently have a structure, I encourage you to embrace the seven parts of the story described here and begin building upon them—or, better yet, create your own structure that makes sense to you.

Regardless, the framework I have described is still just a structure. It's not yet livable. Now it's time for you to put up the drywall, paint the rooms, add furniture, and hang pictures to make the epic narrative your own.

It has been an honor to take this journey with you, and I sincerely hope it will help you appreciate God's relentless love for you. With the rest of your days, may you strengthen the structure and enjoy the mystery.

Acknowledgments

In school, I loved math tests and loathed English assignments. I was incapable of precisely understanding the difference between a "C" paper and an "A" paper. It is, therefore, ironic that I landed on a career as a preacher where I would have to write a six-page essay every week that was evaluated by over a thousand people.

The notion of writing a 250-page book was laughable, so I have numerous people to thank for helping me cross the finish line.

Vicki Kuyper is a professional writer and a personal friend, so I sheepishly sent her my first chapter, wondering if I should continue writing. The chapter was terrible and was eventually rewritten, but Vicki supportively told me to keep writing. Keep writing. Keep writing. She kept telling me to be myself and not try to match the style and pace of other writers. Her words of encouragement were critical, and I would not have finished without them.

I am also thankful for my first readers. Gordon Fuller, Martin Fuller, and Jamie Zack were my young, hip readers who identified references people under thirty would miss. I still think U2 is "current" so I obviously could use all the help I could get. Maggie Brown, Pam Clark, Jim Lyon, and Mark Stoleson were my seasoned Jesus-followers who have collectively read innumerable books. Their gracious questions and thoughtful suggestions certainly made an Overall difference. Lastly, Jason Sauer was my Catholic buddy who had the unenviable task of representing over a billion believers worldwide. I believe he made them proud.

Thank you to Regina, Kevin, and Curt at Warner Press for taking a chance on this unknown, first-time writer. They have been remarkably accommodating as I have poked my nose into areas where it doesn't belong. I'm thankful for their persistent and earnest belief that God could use this book to make a difference in the Kingdom.

Thank you to my kids: Gordon, Martin, and Lila for filling my life with great stories and occasionally giving me permission to share them publicly.

And the last...should be first. My wife, Tami, was the first one who believed I could do this. She was the first one I would seek when I was stuck on a section for days, and she was the first one who read it when I was finished. Tami, you are my first priority and the first one I want to enjoy the Overall story with. I look forward to many more firsts together with you.